Sports Illustrated KIDS

BIG BOOK OF WHO

FOOTBALL

Library of Congress Cataloging-in-Publication Data available upon request.
ISBN 978-1-63727-252-7

Printed and bound in China by RR Donnelley APS

This book is available in quantity at special discounts for your group or organization.

For further information, contact:
Triumph Books LLC
814 North Franklin Street
Chicago, Illinois 60610
(312) 337-0747
www.triumphbooks.com

Produced by
Shoreline Publishing Group LLC
Santa Barbara, California
Designer: Tom Carling, Carling Design Inc.

Updates to 2022 edition text
by James Buckley Jr.

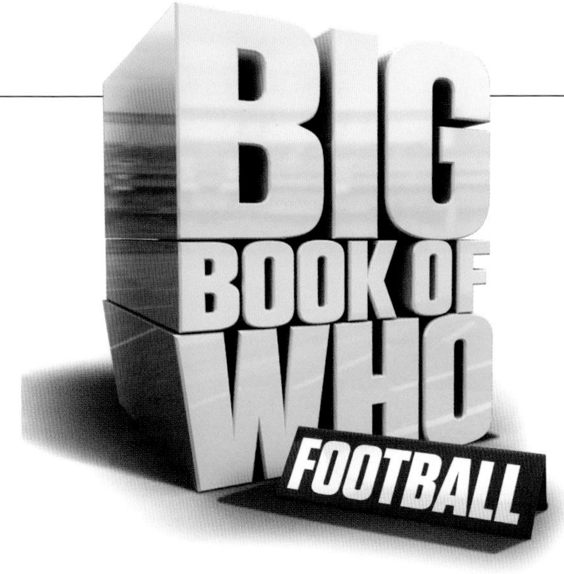

WELCOME

Football is a game of stars. Quarterbacks who complete long passes with pinpoint accuracy, running backs with lightning-quick feet, and defensive stars with the strength to shed blocks before making tackles all help make the NFL the nation's most popular and exciting pro sports league. This book answers questions about many of the game's best players, both past and present. We hope you enjoy it as much as the game itself!

CONTENTS

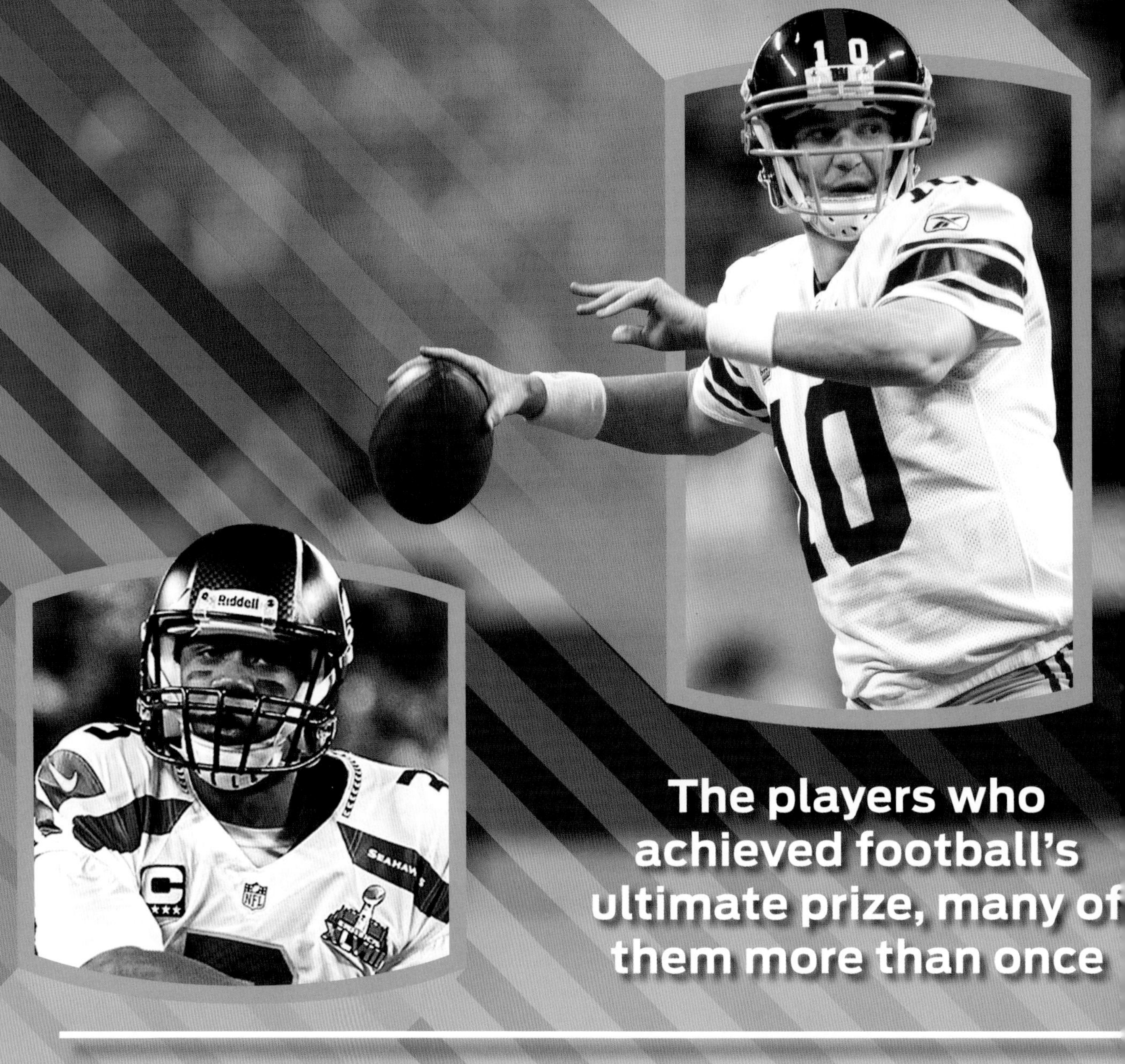

The players who achieved football's ultimate prize, many of them more than once

CHAM

PIONS

Who was the MVP in the Saints' only Super Bowl appearance?

On February 7, 2010, **DREW BREES** led the New Orleans Saints to a 31–17 victory over the Indianapolis Colts in Super Bowl XLIV. He completed 32 of 39 passes for 288 yards and two touchdowns, and was named the game's most valuable player.

The Saints' Super Bowl was very special to New Orleans fans who had endured many losing seasons—the Saints failed to have a winning record in any of the first 20 years they existed! When Hurricane Katrina devastated the city in August 2005, it seemed New Orleans would never have an NFL champion. That's because the team's home stadium, the Louisiana Superdome, suffered so much damage in the storm that many people thought the Saints would have to permanently move to another city.

The Superdome was repaired before the 2006 season, just in time for Brees's first game as a Saint. Three seasons later, the city of New Orleans finally had a Super Bowl champion! When Brees retired after the 2020 season, he was second all-time in touchdown passes (571) and passing yards (80,358).

SUPER STAT

13

THE NFL RECORD NUMBER OF TIMES BREES PASSED FOR 300 OR MORE YARDS IN A GAME DURING THE 2011 SEASON

DID YOU KNOW

FAST FACT: Drew Brees was selected by voters to appear on the cover of EA Sports' Madden NFL 11 video game.

The Saints joined the NFL in 1967, but they won only one playoff game in 39 seasons before Drew Brees became the team's quarterback. New Orleans played in the first Super Bowl in the history of the franchise in 2010. That left only these four NFL teams to have never played in a Super Bowl:

Cleveland Browns

Detroit Lions

Houston Texans

Jacksonville Jaguars

Who was the first player to be named Super Bowl MVP?

Green Bay Packers quarterback **BART STARR** is the original Super Bowl hero. He won MVP honors in each of the first two Super Bowls. The Packers won both games easily, but the road to the second title wasn't so simple. In the 1967 NFL Championship Game, Starr led Green Bay to a last-minute, come-from-behind, 21–17 win over the Dallas Cowboys. "The Ice Bowl" was one of the coldest games ever played (minus-45 wind chill temperatures). The weather was so brutal that one official's whistle froze to his lip!

FAST FACT: Eli Manning set several school records in college at Ole Miss, including overtaking his dad, Archie, in career touchdown passes. Eli threw for 81 scores, 50 more than his father.

Who is the only Giants player to win two Super Bowl MVP Awards?

The MVP of Super Bowls XLII and XLVI was **ELI MANNING**. Both games were come-from-behind wins over the New England Patriots. And both featured remarkable completions to keep game-winning drives alive.

Trailing by four points on his final possession of Super Bowl XLII, in February 2008, Manning escaped the clutches of two Patriots, and launched a pass downfield. Seldom-used receiver **DAVID TYREE** made a remarkable jumping catch, pinning the ball to his helmet with one hand while falling to the ground. Four years later, Manning completed a deep ball along the sidelines to Mario Manningham, who caught it in between two defenders and deftly touched his feet inbounds. Both plays helped lead to Giants wins.

Who was the MVP the last time the Packers won the Super Bowl?

After waiting for three seasons behind superstar QB Brett Favre, **AARON RODGERS** finally got his chance to be the Packers' starting quarterback in 2008. Though the Pack finished 6–10 that season, Rodgers soon turned the team around. He guided Green Bay to an 11–5 record in 2009. The following season, the Packers made it all the way to Super Bowl XLV to face the Pittsburgh Steelers.

Rodgers led the team to a 31–25 victory, the Packers' NFL-best 13th NFL championship. The QB was named the game's MVP after completing 24 of 39 passes for 304 yards and three touchdowns with no interceptions. Both Rodgers and Packers fans certainly agreed that his late arrival as the team's starting quarterback was worth the wait. He has added many more awards since, including NFL MVP titles in 2011, 2014, 2020, and 2021.

SUPER STAT

5

NUMBER OF TIMES GRAHAM LED HIS LEAGUE IN PASSING YARDS, THREE TIMES IN THE AAFC, AND TWICE IN THE NFL

DID YOU KNOW?

Who has the best winning percentage in NFL history as a quarterback?

In his 10-year pro football career, **OTTO GRAHAM** led the Cleveland Browns to a 114–20–4 record and played in his league's title game every season! Cleveland won all four All-America Football Conference (AAFC) championships before the league merged with the NFL in 1950. Many expected the Browns to struggle once they moved to the NFL, but they won the title that season and twice more before Graham retired. Cleveland went 57–13–1 over the six seasons Graham quarterbacked them in the NFL. His winning percentage of 81.4 is a league record.

The Browns lost three close title games in the only years that Graham failed to lead the team to its league's championship. He won three NFL MVP awards in addition to an AAFC MVP and an AAFC co-MVP. Graham's career average of 8.98 yards per pass attempt remains the highest mark in NFL history.

FAST FACT: Otto Graham spent a season in the National Basketball League (now the NBA) before signing with the Cleveland Browns. His Rochester Royals won the NBL championship in 1946.

The Browns were named in 1946 after their first head coach, Paul Brown, who at the time was considered a young football genius. Brown had led nearby Ohio State University to a college football national title in 1942. Known as "The Father of Modern Football," the Hall of Fame coach set lasting trends in the sport with a number of innovations. Among them were using playbooks, introducing the concept of film study, and coming up with the idea to put a radio receiver in the quarterback's helmet so that coaches could talk to the player when he was on the field.

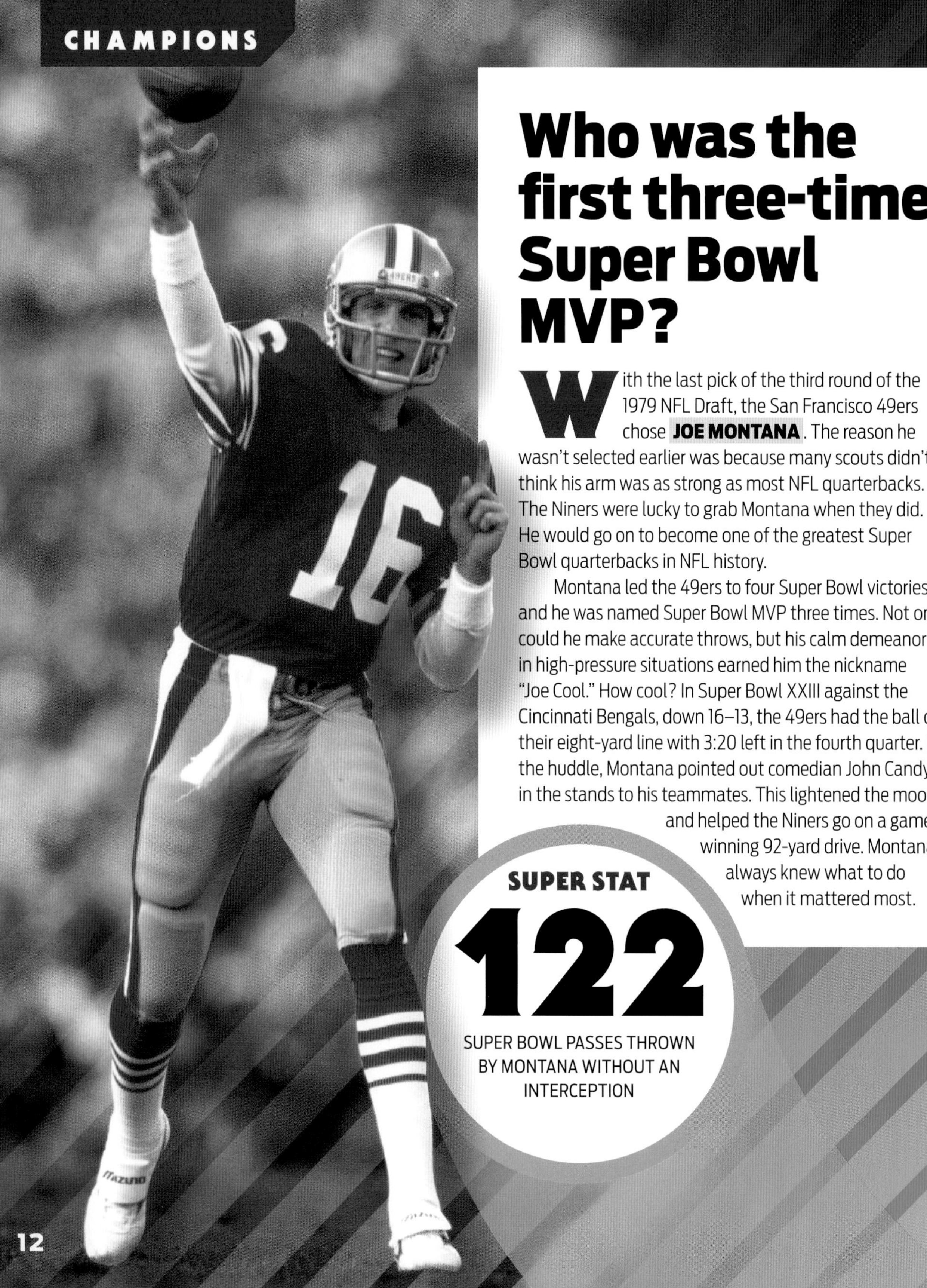

Who was the first three-time Super Bowl MVP?

With the last pick of the third round of the 1979 NFL Draft, the San Francisco 49ers chose **JOE MONTANA**. The reason he wasn't selected earlier was because many scouts didn't think his arm was as strong as most NFL quarterbacks. The Niners were lucky to grab Montana when they did. He would go on to become one of the greatest Super Bowl quarterbacks in NFL history.

Montana led the 49ers to four Super Bowl victories, and he was named Super Bowl MVP three times. Not only could he make accurate throws, but his calm demeanor in high-pressure situations earned him the nickname "Joe Cool." How cool? In Super Bowl XXIII against the Cincinnati Bengals, down 16–13, the 49ers had the ball on their eight-yard line with 3:20 left in the fourth quarter. In the huddle, Montana pointed out comedian John Candy in the stands to his teammates. This lightened the mood and helped the Niners go on a game-winning 92-yard drive. Montana always knew what to do when it mattered most.

SUPER STAT

122

SUPER BOWL PASSES THROWN BY MONTANA WITHOUT AN INTERCEPTION

SUPER STAT

1

NUMBER OF PLAYOFF APPEARANCES THE STEELERS MADE IN THEIR 35-YEAR HISTORY BEFORE BRADSHAW JOINED THE TEAM

Who was the first quarterback to win the Super Bowl four times?

After a standout college career at Louisiana Tech, **TERRY BRADSHAW** was the first overall draft pick in 1970. However, NFL success did not come easy. He struggled so badly that he was even benched in his fifth season. Once he regained his starting spot in October of that season, Bradshaw led the Pittsburgh Steelers to Super Bowl IX, in 1975, where they beat the Minnesota Vikings for the team's first title.

Bradshaw improved dramatically the next season, leading the Steelers to a second straight Super Bowl win, this time over the Dallas Cowboys. He would lead Pittsburgh once more to back-to-back Super Bowls four years later, against the Cowboys (again) and the Los Angeles Rams. Bradshaw was MVP of both of those games.

Who led his team to three comeback postseason wins in a row?

Kansas City Chiefs quarterback **PATRICK MAHOMES** must have studied drama in college. Because during the playoffs for the 2019 NFL season, he certainly put on a show, while keeping fans on the edge of their seats.

In the divisional round, the Chiefs fell behind the Houston Texas 24–0 only five minutes into the second quarter! Few teams have ever come back from that far behind. But few teams have a comeback king like Mahomes. He proceeded to throw four touchdown passes in the quarter, including three to tight end Travis Kelce, and the Chiefs held the halftime lead, 28–24. Kansas City kept rolling in the second half and ended up winning 51–31.

In the AFC Championship Game, the comeback was not as dramatic, but it was a comeback. The Tennessee Titans were on top 17–7 when Mahomes worked his magic. He threw a TD pass to Tyreek Hill and then carried the ball in himself on a 27-yard run to take the lead. Kansas City sealed the deal in the second half and won 35-24 to earn a spot in Super Bowl LIV.

In that game, Kansas City once again fell behind, this time 20–10 late in the third quarter to the San Francisco 49ers. But Mahomes had done it before, so he did it again. He hit Kelce with a TD pass and then led a drive to a TD run by Damien Williams to take the lead with less than three minutes to go. A final Williams TD created the 31–20 final score.

SUPER STAT

50

THE NUMBER OF TD PASSES MAHOMES THREW IN 2018, TYING TOM BRADY FOR SECOND-MOST ALL-TIME FOR A SINGLE SEASON

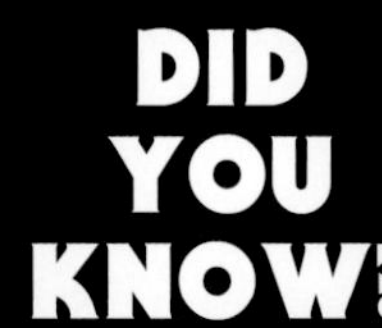

FAST FACT: In 2020, Mahomes threw his 100th career touchdown pass. It was a 28-yard bullet to Tyreek Hill, and came in Mahomes's 40th NFL game, setting a new record for fastest to reach the century mark.

Patrick Mahomes has had a pretty spectacular NFL career, with four Pro Bowl selections, a Super Bowl MVP, and the 2018 AP Offensive Player of the Year Award. But he was good enough in another sport that he might have racked up trophies there, too. Mahomes's father, Patrick Sr., pitched in the Major Leagues for 11 seasons. Patrick grew up learning to throw from a pro! Patrick was a standout high school baseball player and was even drafted by the Detroit Tigers in the 2014 MLB Amateur Draft. Though he doesn't play baseball, he does own a small part of the Kansas City Royals.

Who completed the highest percentage of passes in one Super Bowl?

The New York Giants' **PHIL SIMMS** completed 22 of 25 pass attempts (88 percent) in Super Bowl XXI, in 1987. He had as many touchdown passes as incompletions, and two of the three incompletions were drops by receivers. The Giants won their first Super Bowl title, and Simms was MVP.

After the game, Simms became the first of many athletes to say the now-famous line, "I'm going to Disney World!" This ad campaign was set up to work no matter which team won the game. If Denver had won instead, Broncos quarterback John Elway would have said the line.

SUPER STAT

30

POINTS SCORED BY THE GIANTS AFTER HALFTIME IN SUPER BOWL XXI, TURNING AN EARLY DEFICIT INTO A LOPSIDED 39–20 WIN

FAST FACT: Emmitt Smith carried the ball more often (4,409 attempts) for more yards (18,355 yards) and more touchdowns (164) than any other running back in NFL history.

Who has rushed for the most career touchdowns in Super Bowl history?

The Dallas Cowboys beat the Pittsburgh Steelers, 27–17, in Super Bowl XXX, in January 1996. The Cowboys became the first team to win three Super Bowls in a four-year span. It was the legs of a running back named **EMMITT SMITH** that carried them there.

Smith's two touchdowns against the Steelers were the fourth and fifth Super Bowl rushing touchdowns of his career, the most ever. He scored at least once in all three Super Bowls in which he played. Smith found the end zone when it mattered most: All five of his Super Bowl touchdowns came in the second half of games.

Who has the most rushing TDs in one Super Bowl?

For almost the entire second quarter of Super Bowl XXXII, in 1998, **TERRELL DAVIS** of the Broncos was on the bench with a blinding migraine headache. Thanks to emergency treatment on the sideline, Davis was able to return for the second half and wound up rushing for 157 yards and a Super Bowl-record three touchdowns in his team's 31–24 win over the Green Bay Packers. It was Denver's first victory in five trips to the Super Bowl.

SUPER STAT

17

NUMBER OF INTERCEPTIONS STAFFORD THREW IN 2021 TO LEAD THE NFL; WINNING THE SUPER BOWL MADE UP FOR THAT!

FAST FACT: Stafford had a rough start to his NFL career. Injuries cost him games in 2009 and 2010. So when he led the NFL with 663 pass attempts in 2011, he was named the NFL Comeback Player of the Year.

Who had the most career passing yards before winning his first Super Bowl?

In 12 seasons with the Detroit Lions, quarterback **MATTHEW STAFFORD** had eight seasons with 4,000 or more yards passing. He threw for more than 280 touchdowns. But he never earned a championship ring. In 2021, he joined the Los Angeles Rams and added more yards and TDs, finally reaching 49,995 yards and 323 TD passes by the time the playoffs began. No one had ever racked up those numbers without winning a title. Stafford was about to change that. Surrounded by more talent than he ever had in Detroit, he led the Rams to four straight playoff wins, including a dramatic, come-from-behind 20–17 victory in the NFC Championship Game. Against Cincinnati In Super Bowl LVI, Stafford was solid again, throwing three touchdown passes. The last came with less than 90 seconds left, a one-yard strike to Cooper Kupp for the winning points in L.A.'s 23–20 win.

DID YOU KNOW?

Before 2011, only Dan Marino (5,084 in 1984) and Drew Brees (5,069 in 2008) had topped 5,000 passing yards in a season. In 2011, Matthew Stafford was one of three players to beat that mark with 5,038, but at 23, he was the youngest. Tom Brady (34) had 5,235 while Drew Brees (32) had 5,476.

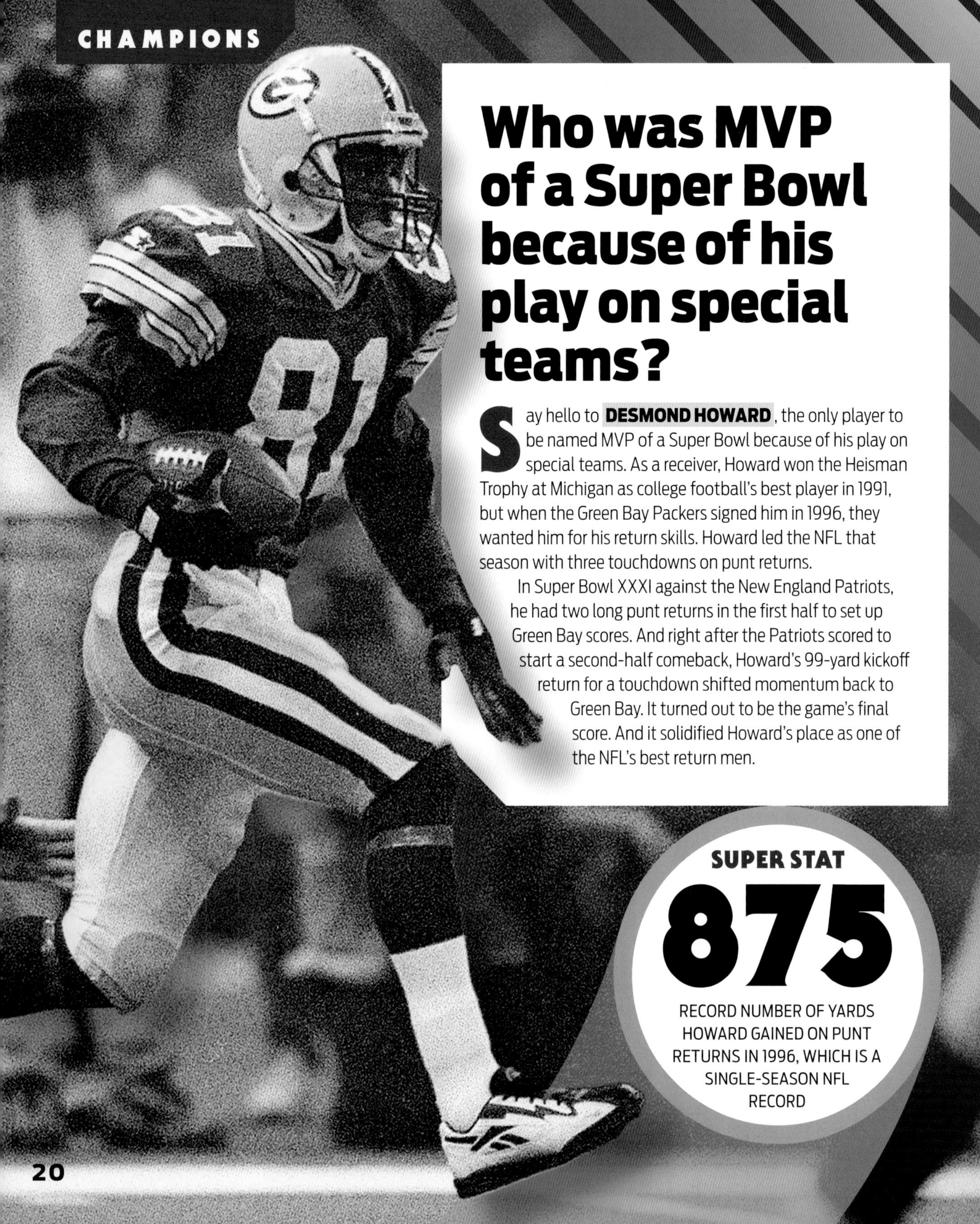

Who was MVP of a Super Bowl because of his play on special teams?

Say hello to **DESMOND HOWARD**, the only player to be named MVP of a Super Bowl because of his play on special teams. As a receiver, Howard won the Heisman Trophy at Michigan as college football's best player in 1991, but when the Green Bay Packers signed him in 1996, they wanted him for his return skills. Howard led the NFL that season with three touchdowns on punt returns.

In Super Bowl XXXI against the New England Patriots, he had two long punt returns in the first half to set up Green Bay scores. And right after the Patriots scored to start a second-half comeback, Howard's 99-yard kickoff return for a touchdown shifted momentum back to Green Bay. It turned out to be the game's final score. And it solidified Howard's place as one of the NFL's best return men.

SUPER STAT

875

RECORD NUMBER OF YARDS HOWARD GAINED ON PUNT RETURNS IN 1996, WHICH IS A SINGLE-SEASON NFL RECORD

SUPER STAT

5

THE RECORD NUMBER OF SUPER BOWL MVP AWARDS WON BY BRADY IN HIS 10 SUPER BOWLS (ALSO A RECORD FOR MOST PLAYED)

Who threw for the most yards in one Super Bowl?

Megastar QB **TOM BRADY** has all the other passing records for career Super Bowl performances, why not this single-game mark? In Super Bowl LII, Brady threw for 505 yards. He broke the old record of 466 yards . . . that he had set himself a year earlier! As the Pats battled the Philadelphia Eagles in LII, Brady completed 28 of 48 attempts and threw three TD passes. He was just continuing one of his best seasons, statistically. Including 11 games in which he threw for 250 or more yards, he led the NFL with 581 attempts and 4,577 passing yards on his way to winning the NFL MVP award and his 13th Pro Bowl selection. In two playoff games, he threw five TDs with no interceptions. Brady started hot in the Super Bowl, as did Nick Foles of the Eagles. After a Brady TD pass gave New England a late lead, Foles rallied Philly to score the final 10 points of the game for a 41–33 upset win. Knowing Brady, he'd trade the record for another ring in a hearbeat.

SUPER STAT

11

NUMBER OF TD PASSES FLACCO THREW DURING THE PLAYOFFS THAT FOLLOWED THE 2012 SEASON, WITH NO INTERCEPTIONS

FAST FACT: Joe Flacco was the first quarterback in NFL history to win at least one playoff game in each of his first five pro seasons.

Who was MVP the last time the Ravens reached the Super Bowl?

The playoffs following the 2012 NFL regular season were one big **JOE FLACCO** party. After his Baltimore Ravens beat the Indianapolis Colts, he led his team to Denver to face the AFC's top-seeded Broncos. That's where Flacco completed a game-tying 70-yard touchdown pass to Jacoby Jones with less than a minute remaining in the fourth quarter. The play became known as the "Flacco Fling."

The Ravens went on to beat the Broncos in overtime, then upset the New England Patriots the following week in the AFC Championship Game. Two weeks later, Flacco faced the San Francisco 49ers in Super Bowl XLVII. He built a 21–3 lead with three touchdown passes in the first half, and would finish the game with 287 passing yards. His ability to avoid throwing an interception helped secure the 34–31 win and MVP honors.

DID YOU KNOW?

Flacco is the oldest of six children from a very athletic family. His brother Mike was selected by the Baltimore Orioles in the 2009 MLB Amateur Draft, his brother John was a wide receiver at Stanford, and brother Tom was a college QB as well. Sister Stephanie was a field hockey and basketball star in high school.

Who has thrown the most touchdown passes in one Super Bowl?

QB **STEVE YOUNG** overcame a career of frustration when he set a Super Bowl record with six TD passes to help the San Francisco 49ers crush the San Diego Chargers, 49–26, in Super Bowl XXIX, in January 1995. After having started his NFL career with just three wins in two seasons with the Tampa Bay Buccaneers, Young was traded to San Francisco. He then spent four years backing up the great Joe Montana. Even after taking over for Montana, Young lost two straight NFC Championship Games to the Dallas Cowboys. But he broke through the following year by beating the Cowboys in the Championship Game, and then the Chargers in the Super Bowl.

Who has kicked the most Super Bowl-winning field goals?

How do you earn the nickname "Mr. Clutch"? Just do what **ADAM VINATIERI** did. First, during Super Bowl XXXVI, the St. Louis Rams tied the game late in the fourth quarter. Vinatieri's New England Patriots drove to set up his field goal try. He made the 48-yard kick as time expired to become the first player to score on a Super Bowl's final play. Two years later, he made a 41-yard field goal with four seconds left to beat the Carolina Panthers in the Super Bowl . . . again! That's how you earn a famous nickname!

Who has scored the longest touchdown by a defensive player in a Super Bowl?

The Pittsburgh Steelers' **JAMES HARRISON** returned an interception 100 yards for a key score in Super Bowl XLIII, in Feburary 2009. When the Arizona Cardinals had the ball on the Steelers' 1-yard line late in the first half, Harrison crept up toward the line, and the Cards assumed he'd be blitzing. Instead, Harrison faked a blitz and backpedaled in front of the intended target — receiver Anquan Boldin. Harrison caught the pass on his goal line and took off down the right sideline.

Harrison was tackled by Larry Fitzgerald just as he reached his 100th yard, scoring as time expired in the first half. While chasing him, Fitzgerald had run into his own teammate, preventing Fitzgerald from making the tackle earlier in the play. An exhausted Harrison lay on the ground in the end zone for a while, then returned to the bench and immediately used an oxygen mask to catch his breath!

SUPER STAT

19

NUMBER OF DEFENSIVE TOUCHDOWNS SCORED IN ALL SUPER BOWLS (THROUGH LVI IN 2022)

SUPER STAT

18

NUMBER OF CAREER TOUCHDOWNS THAT BRADY HAS THROWN IN THE SUPER BOWL, THE MOST EVER BY A QUARTERBACK

FAST FACT: Tom Brady played catcher for his high school's baseball team and was selected in the 18th round of the 1995 MLB Amateur Draft by the Montreal Expos. (The Expos moved to Washington in 2005 and became the Nationals.)

Who has the most career passing yards in Super Bowl history?

It took a lot of determination and luck for **TOM BRADY** to crack the starting lineup, but he's been a star ever since. He was not chosen until the sixth round of the 2000 NFL Draft by the New England Patriots. He didn't become the team's starter until 2001. Then, of course, he led them to their first Super Bowl win, 20-17 over the St. Louis Rams. Brady was named the game's Most Valuable Player. It was the start of the NFL's most remarkable career.

Brady and the Patriots won Super Bowl XXXVIII (2003 season) and Super Bowl XXXIX (2004). After reaching two more Super Bowls and losing both to the New York Giants, in February 2015, Brady led the Patriots to their fourth Super Bowl victory and took home his third MVP award. In February 2017, he led the greatest comeback in Super Bowl history, earning another MVP trophy as the Patriots beat the Atlanta Falcons in overtime. He won his sixth Super Bowl, the most ever by a player, with a win over the L.A. Rams after the 2019 season. Finally, after moving to the Tampa Bay Buccaneers, Brady made it lucky seven (and five MVPs) in a win over Kansas City. His all-time No. 1 total in the big game? 3,039 passing yards.

DID YOU KNOW?

While Brady has been pretty awesome in the Super Bowl, he's done pretty well in the regular season as well. He has led the NFL in touchdown passs five times, including 50 in 2007, then a record and still tied for second-most all-time, and 43 in 2021, when he was 44 years old. He was also tops in passing yards in 2021 with 5,316, a career-best in his 22nd season. He was by far the oldest QB to do any of those things. Even though he retired for a month, he came back in 2022 and was ready to add to his remarkable stats.

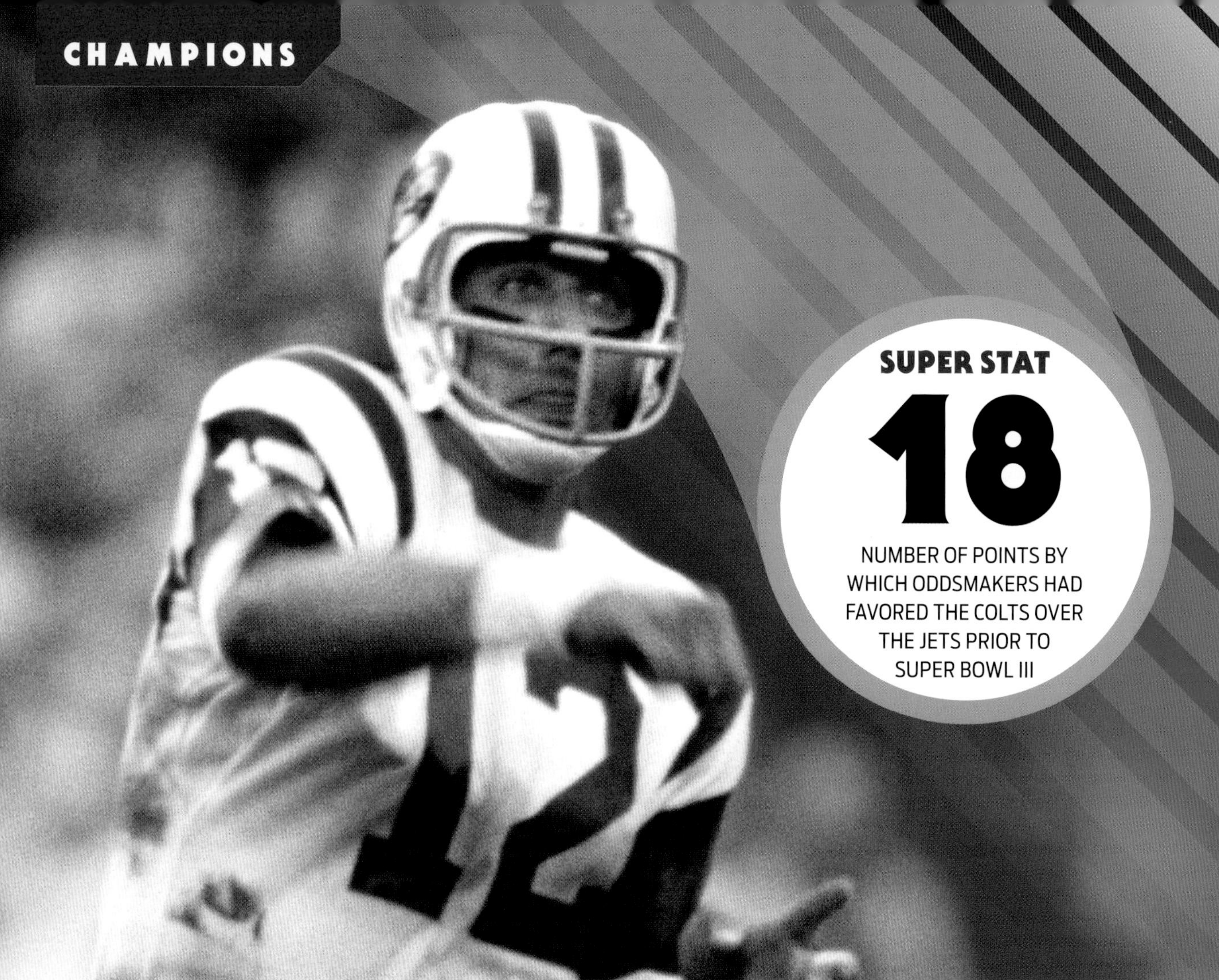

SUPER STAT

18

NUMBER OF POINTS BY WHICH ODDSMAKERS HAD FAVORED THE COLTS OVER THE JETS PRIOR TO SUPER BOWL III

Who quarterbacked the team that pulled off the biggest Super Bowl upset?

New York Jets QB **JOE NAMATH** led the New York Jets to a shocking 16–7 win over the Baltimore Colts in Super Bowl III, in January 1969. Few people expected the AFL's Jets to win. The NFL's Colts had lost one game all season and were coming off a 34–0 shutout of the Cleveland Browns. Namath, meanwhile, had thrown more interceptions than touchdowns that season. The NFL's Packers had also handily beaten the AFL entrant in the first two Super Bowls, so most people thought that proved the NFL's superiority to the AFL. Still, Namath famously guaranteed a Jets upset victory, making headlines and enraging his coach. Namath had the last laugh.

SUPER STAT

75

NUMBER OF GAMES WON BY RUSSELL WILSON IN HIS FIRST SEVEN SEASONS, THE MOST BY A QB IN NFL HISTORY

Who led the Seahawks to their only Super Bowl title?

Although **RUSSELL WILSON** was traded to the Denver Broncos before the 2022 season, he'll always be remembered in Seattle for being the driving force behind the Seahawks' only Super Bowl win. With a total team effort, Seattle smashed the highly favored Denver Broncos 43–8 in Super Bowl XLVIII. Wilson had a lot of help, of course, including bruising running back Marshawn Lynch and the Legion of Boom defense. Linebacker Malcolm Smith was a particular standout. After making an interception in the closing minute of the NFC Championship Game, Smith followed that up by picking off Denver quarterback Peyton Manning and returning the ball for a 69-yard touchdown in the main event. Smith was named the game's MVP, but Wilson emerged as the team's biggest star.

Players who are known for more than just the way they played the game on the field

PERSON

ALITIES

FAST FACT: Henry was the second of four Alabama players to earn the Heisman. The others: RB Mark Ingram (2009); WR DeVonta Smith (2020); and QB Bryce Young (2021).

DID YOU KNOW

SUPER STAT

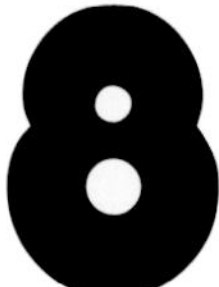

8

INCLUDING HENRY, THE NUMBER OF PLAYERS WHO HAVE RUSHED FOR 2,000 OR MORE YARDS IN A SINGLE NFL SESAON

What two-time NFL rushing leader was also a Heisman Trophy winner?

Winning the Heisman Trophy as college football's best player does not always mean the winner will become an NFL star. In the case of **DERRICK HENRY**, it was a sure signal. Henry set an SEC record for rushing yards on the way to winning the Heisman in 2015 for Alabama. Surprisingly, he was not selected until the second round of the 2016 NFL Draft by the Tennessee Titans. Henry was not a starter for most of his first two seasons. In 2018, he finally got a chance and topped 1,000 yards for the first time. A highlight of that season was an NFL-record-tying 99-yard touchdown run.

In 2019, Henry broke out in a big way. He led the NFL with 1,540 yards, 303 carries, and 16 rushing TDs. That season was awesome, but his 2020 year was even better. The big back rambled for 2,027 yards, the fifth-highest total all-time. His 17 TDs led the league again. He was named the AP Offensive Player of the Year.

Derrick Henry was surprised that scouts did not put him among the best players in the 2016 NFL Draft. Some said he was too slow or too big for the NFL game. He was upset by the pre-draft grades he received. "Nobody is going to outwork me," Henry said. "I feel fee like hard work pushes you over the limit and makes you who you are. I'm going to work hard every day." The Titans picked him to back up DeMarco Murray, for whom they had just traded. It was not long before Henry pushed Murray aside to earn the starting role. For Titans fans, he was worth the wait!

Who was "the Punky QB"?

Quarterbacks have a reputation for being stars beloved by all. They smile at reporters, sign autographs, and work to become leaders. But sometimes you need something different. That's what the Chicago Bears got in 1985 with **JIM McMAHON**. Tall, loud, and not afraid to make waves, McMahon was the perfect QB for the Bears' defense- and rushing-led team. McMahon's punky style made headlines, but he won every game he started. In the playoffs, he threw three TDs and rushed for three more. Chicago won Super Bowl XX 46–10 over the Patriots.

FAST FACT: Boomer Esiason won the NFL MVP award in 1988.

Who was the NFL quarterback known as "Boomer"?

Sometimes, people get nicknames early in life. Such was the case for **NORMAN "BOOMER" ESIASON**. While his mother was still pregnant with him, his father felt her belly and was surprised by the power he felt. "He must be a boomer because he kicks so much," Esiason's father said. But becoming a kicker was not in the cards for Boomer.

Instead, Esiason ended up throwing passes as a star quarterback. He was best known for his mastery of Cincinnati Bengals head coach Sam Wyche's no-huddle offense. The team rode that offense all the way to Super Bowl XXIII, in January 1989, which the Bengals narrowly lost, 20–16, to the San Francisco 49ers.

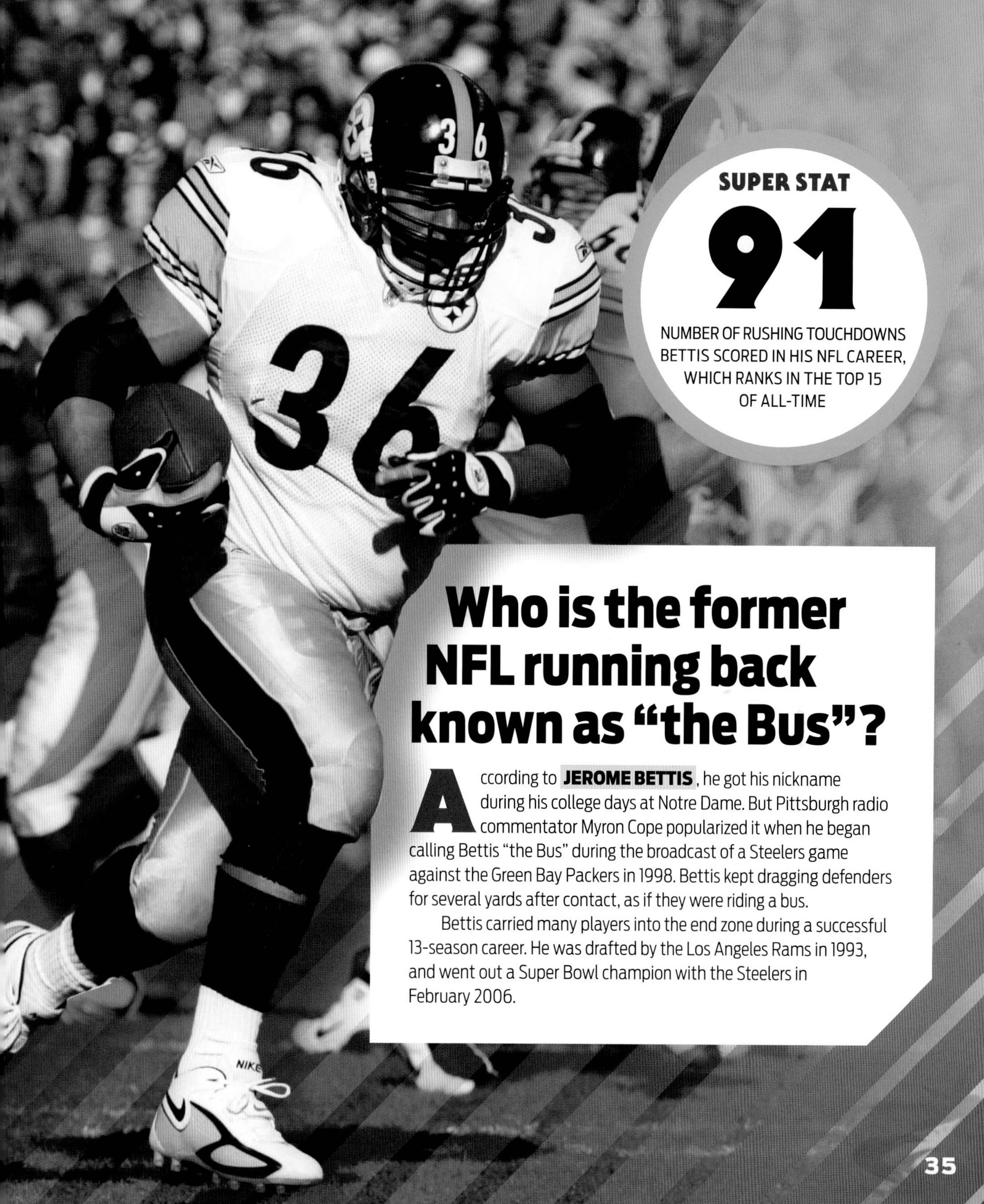

SUPER STAT

91

NUMBER OF RUSHING TOUCHDOWNS BETTIS SCORED IN HIS NFL CAREER, WHICH RANKS IN THE TOP 15 OF ALL-TIME

Who is the former NFL running back known as "the Bus"?

According to **JEROME BETTIS**, he got his nickname during his college days at Notre Dame. But Pittsburgh radio commentator Myron Cope popularized it when he began calling Bettis "the Bus" during the broadcast of a Steelers game against the Green Bay Packers in 1998. Bettis kept dragging defenders for several yards after contact, as if they were riding a bus.

Bettis carried many players into the end zone during a successful 13-season career. He was drafted by the Los Angeles Rams in 1993, and went out a Super Bowl champion with the Steelers in February 2006.

SUPER STAT

60

THE RECORD NUMBER OF TD PASSES BURROW THREW FOR LSU IN 2019 (A RECORD SINCE TOPPED BY BAILEY ZAPPE IN 2021)

What NFL QB is a huge fan of Spongebob Squarepants?

Are you ready, kids . . . to find out the answer to this question? Cincinnati Bengals star QB **JOE BURROW** would be happy to sing you the answer! After an outstanding, national-championship career at LSU, Burrow joined the Bengals as the first overall draft pick in 2020. He quickly showed that he was the right pick, leading the Bengals to the Super Bowl in only his second season. Along with a strong passing arm, Burrow showed a leadership rare among young players. He also became one of the NFL's most popular personalities. One reason was his love of the yellow cartoon hero from under the sea. Burrow wore Spongebob socks to the Heisman Trophy ceremony and was seen with a Squidward hat after a win. After another game, he wore a Krusty Krab sweatshirt. In 2021, he was even slimed by a fellow player after being named the Nickelodeon MVP!

DID YOU KNOW

FAST FACT: In a 2021 game against the Baltimore Ravens, Burrow threw for 525 yards, the fourth-highest single-game total in NFL history.

Joe Burrow has roots in pro football in two countries. In the early 1970s, his father, Jimmy, played defensive back for the University of Nebraska. After a few games with the Green Bay Packers, Jimmy moved to the Montreal Alouettes of the Canadian Football League. He helped them win the Grey Cup, the CFL championship, in 1977. After his playing career, he coached in the Arena Football League and in college football for many years.

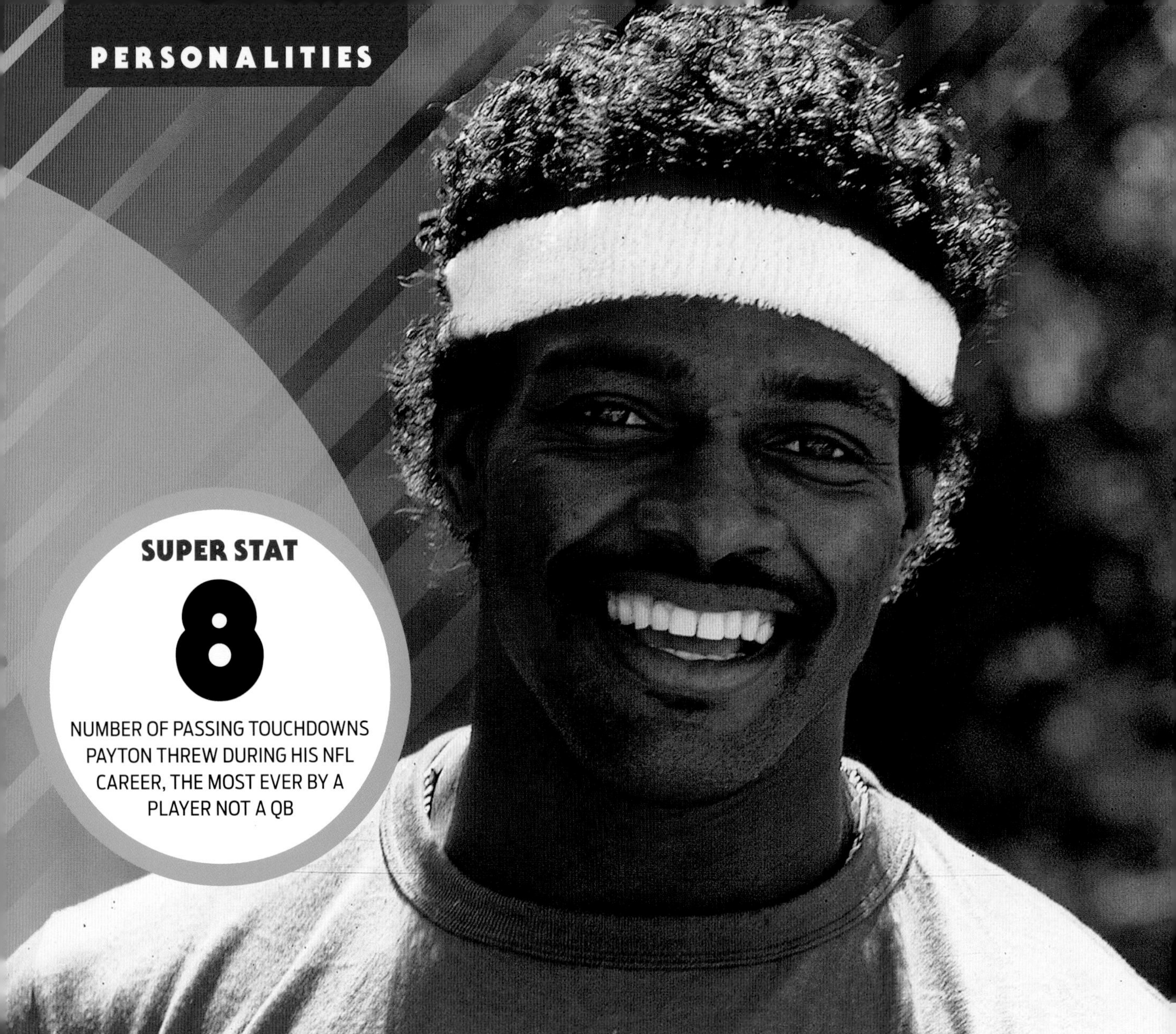

SUPER STAT

8

NUMBER OF PASSING TOUCHDOWNS PAYTON THREW DURING HIS NFL CAREER, THE MOST EVER BY A PLAYER NOT A QB

Who was the NFL running back known as "Sweetness"?

How did **WALTER PAYTON** of the Chicago Bears earn his nickname? To be honest, no one is certain. While some say it was his grace on the field, others cite his easygoing personality off it. The name could be ironic, since Payton was aggressive on the field, often dishing out as much punishment as he took.

For all the wear and tear, Payton was remarkably durable. His 170 consecutive starts between 1975 and '87 are the most ever for a running back. Payton was the 1977 NFL MVP who owned many big records when he retired. Emmitt Smith broke his career rushing record of 16,726 yards. Corey Dillon first broke his single-game mark of 275 rushing yards.

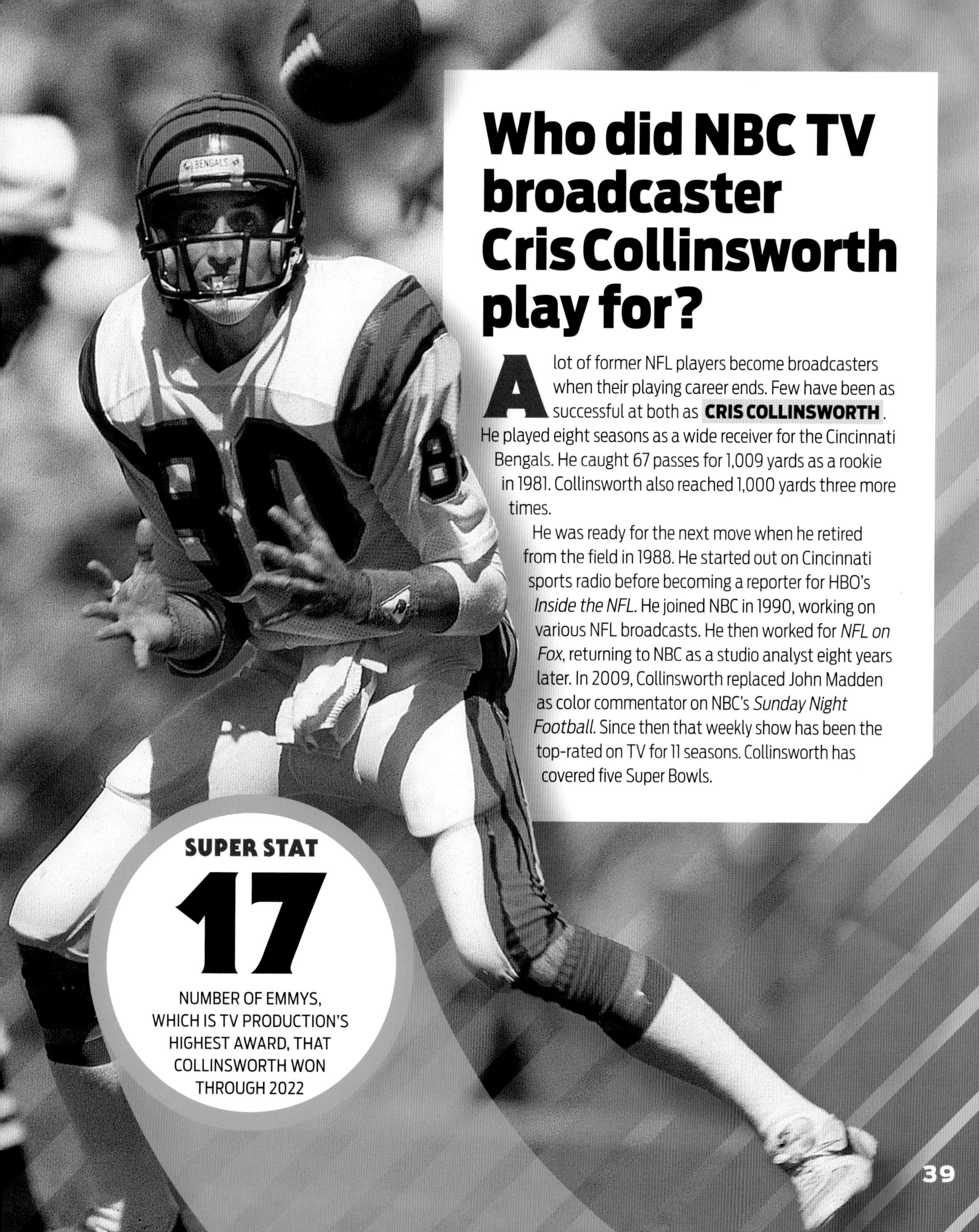

Who did NBC TV broadcaster Cris Collinsworth play for?

A lot of former NFL players become broadcasters when their playing career ends. Few have been as successful at both as **CRIS COLLINSWORTH**. He played eight seasons as a wide receiver for the Cincinnati Bengals. He caught 67 passes for 1,009 yards as a rookie in 1981. Collinsworth also reached 1,000 yards three more times.

He was ready for the next move when he retired from the field in 1988. He started out on Cincinnati sports radio before becoming a reporter for HBO's *Inside the NFL*. He joined NBC in 1990, working on various NFL broadcasts. He then worked for *NFL on Fox*, returning to NBC as a studio analyst eight years later. In 2009, Collinsworth replaced John Madden as color commentator on NBC's *Sunday Night Football*. Since then that weekly show has been the top-rated on TV for 11 seasons. Collinsworth has covered five Super Bowls.

SUPER STAT

17

NUMBER OF EMMYS, WHICH IS TV PRODUCTION'S HIGHEST AWARD, THAT COLLINSWORTH WON THROUGH 2022

SUPER STAT

WAYS SANDERS SCORED TOUCHDOWNS: RUSHING; RECEIVING; INTERCEPTION, FUMBLE, KICKOFF, AND PUNT RETURNS

Who is known as "Prime Time"?

As a player, **DEION SANDERS** was a larger-than-life personality. He was known for brash statements about his outstanding abilities, but he backed it up with excellent play on the field. Sanders's trademark move was the high-step, which he performed as he neared the end zone. He would put one hand behind his head and hold the football outstretched in his other as he pranced toward the goal line.

Sanders was labeled "Prime Time" in high school after showcasing his basketball moves in games played during the prime-time TV hours. He lived up to the name during a 14-year NFL career for five teams: the Atlanta Falcons, San Francisco 49ers, Dallas Cowboys, Washington Redskins, and Baltimore Ravens. His 1,331 career yards on interception returns ranks fourth in NFL history,. Sanders won Super Bowls with the 49ers and Cowboys. In 2020, he became head coach at Jackson State, a historically Black college in Mississippi. He led them to an 11–1 record and a conference title and was named the national coach of the year for the Football Championship Subdivision.

DID YOU KNOW?

FAST FACT: Deion Sanders is the only athlete to play in both a Super Bowl and a World Series.

Deion Sanders was such a great athlete that he played Major League Baseball during the same time that he played in the NFL. He suited up for the four teams shown here over nine big league seasons. His best season was 1992, when he hit .304 with 14 triples and 26 steals for the Atlanta Braves.

New York Yankees

Atlanta Braves

Cincinnati Reds

San Francisco Giants

Which team's stadium is home to the Dawg Pound?

For many seasons, fans of the **CLEVELAND BROWNS** did not have much to cheer for. Then, in the mid-1980s, the team reached the playoffs five seasons in a row, 1985 through 1989. In 1985, two members of the secondary took to calling teammates "Dawgs." In fact, they even put up a sign at Cleveland Stadium naming one part of the bleachers the Dawg Pound. Fans there took to the nickname with glee. Dog masks soon appeared. Fans tossed biscuits at players who made big plays. Many choruses of "Woofs!" were heard. The Dawg Pound flourished during the team's playoff run. Though the team has not neared those heights since, the devoted Dawg Pound continues to bark.

What team's fans are known as Cheeseheads?

Wisconsin is home to tens of thousands of dairy cows. Their milk is used to produce dozens of types of tasty cheese. So when Chicago Bears fans began mocking **GREEN BAY PACKERS** fans by calling them Cheeseheads after their state's most famous product... the folks in Green Bay were not insulted. In fact, one creative fellow decided to celebrate the nickname. In 1987, Ralph Bruno carved a piece of yellow foam into a cheesy wedge and wore it proudly on his head. His creations caught on and Cheeseheads began appearing regularly in the stands at Lambeau Field. By 1993, the Packers were once again appearing regularly in the playoffs and their foam-topped fans got national attention they've enjoyed ever since.

Who was known as "The Boz"?

As a college linebacker with the University of Oklahoma, **BRIAN BOSWORTH** was one of the best. He earned two Butkus Awards as the nation's top LB and helped Oklahoma win the 1985 national title. With him leading a punishing defense, the Sooners lost only four games while he was there. Part of his fame also came from his oversized personality and famous nickname: The Boz. He colored his hair, boasted of his skills, and earned attention on and off the field. Injuries limited his NFL career to only three seasons, however.

Who performed the "Ickey Shuffle"?

Sometimes rookies make a name for themselves with their great play. Other times, they are fresh personalities on the NFL scene. In 1988, Cincinnati Bengals running back **ICKEY WOODS** was both. A second-round draft pick from UNLV, Woods first leaped to national attention in Week 4. He scored his first two NFL touchdowns and debuted a hopping, shuffling, ball-spiking end zone dance that quickly became nationally famous. Woods just kept scoring—and dancing—eventually leading the AFC with 15 rushing TDs. His joy at every score, along with his big smile and bubbly personality, made him a media star. The Bengals advanced to Super Bowl XXIII, where they lost to the San Francisco 49ers. No scoring—or dancing—for Woods in that game. He only played until 1991, but his famous dance lives on.

FAST FACT: Woods's real first name is Elbert. He got his famous nickname when his younger brother had trouble saying Elbert. It came out as "Ee-ee," which family members changed to Ickey.

SUPER STAT

5.3

THE AVERAGE NUMBER OF RUSHING YARDS PER ATTEMPT BY WOODS IN 1988, WHICH LED THE NFL

Which Ravens defender danced before his home games?

Few players played the game with such zeal and relish as Baltimore Ravens linebacker **RAY LEWIS**. From his first season in 1996, he was was a team leader, famed for his fierce tackling as well as his inspirational speeches. A star at the University of Miami, where he set records for tackles, Lewis was the Ravens' first-round pick in 1996. He became a starter almost right away. By his second season, he was setting NFL records (see Super Stat) and had earned the first of his 12 Pro Bowl selections.

Lewis started another tradition, leading the defense out of the tunnel before each home game and performing a sliding, leaping, shouting dance he called "The Squirrel." Lewis later said that he had been in a teenage dance group when he learned the moves. Looking for something to get his team excited, he debuted the dance and it became a tradition. One part of the dance was tossing hunks of grass in the air. That became a problem when the Ravens' stadium switched to artificial turf. The problem was solved by putting a small patch of grass near the tunnel for Lewis to grab on his way out!

Lewis and the Ravens had their most danceworthy season in 2000, when the defense had nine games with fewer than 10 points allowed, including four shutouts. The trend continued in the playoffs, as they allowed only 23 points in four wins. The last was a 34–7 victory over the New York Giants for the Ravens' first Super Bowl title.

FAST FACT: Lewis is one of four linebackers to be named Super Bowl MVP. The others are: Chuck Howley (1971); Malcolm Smith (2014); and Von Miller (2016).

SUPER STAT

156

NFL-RECORD NUMBER OF SOLO TACKLES LEWIS RECORDED IN 1997

Who once changed his name to match the number he wore?

Wide receiver **CHAD JOHNSON** averaged nearly 80 catches per season over seven years with the Cincinnati Bengals. He was known just as well, however, for his antics off the field.

Before the 2008 season, Johnson legally changed his last name to Ochocinco. He did it to highlight a nickname he had created for himself based on his Number 85 jersey. In Spanish, *ocho* is the number eight and *cinco* is five. Regardless of what fans thought of Johnson's quirks, he certainly kept people entertained. He once outraced a horse for charity, and in 2011 he rode a 1,500-pound bull named Déjà Blu (for 1.5 seconds) in a Professional Bull Riding event.

SUPER STAT

66

TEAM-RECORD NUMBER OF TOUCHDOWN PASSES JOHNSON CAUGHT OVER 10 SEASONS WITH THE CINCINNATI BENGALS

SUPER STAT

8

THE NUMBER OF DEFENSIVE BACKS, INCLUDING MATHIEU, INCLUDED ON THE PRO FOOTBALL HALL OF FAME'S ALL-2010s TEAM

Who is known as the "Honey Badger"?

The real honey badger is a mammal about the size of a small dog that lives in Africa and Asia. Though small, it's extremely fierce, active, and feisty. It will take on prey larger than itself, and its tough skin means it can ignore bee stings while pursuing insect larvae. So why is New Orleans Saints defensive back **TYRANN MATHIEU** nicknamed for these wild animals? It started when he was a ball-hawking safety for the LSU Tigers. He specialized in creating turnovers, forcing 11 fumbles in his two seasons there. After one game, a coach saw a viral video of a honey badger leaping out in a wild-and-crazy way. He said the animal's antics reminded him of how Mathieu went all-out on the field. Within days, the nickname had stuck. Mathieu finished fifth in the Heisman Trophy voting and became a rookie starter for the Arizona Cardinals in 2013. Mathieu joined the Kansas City Chiefs in 2019 and helped them win a Super Bowl. In 2022, he joined the Saints.

SUPER STAT

3

NUMBER OF NFL SEASONS IN WHICH JACKSON HAD THE LONGEST RUN FROM SCRIMMAGE

Who was an All-Star in baseball and a Pro Bowl running back?

Sports fans around the world learned what "Bo Knows" in the 1980s when multitalented athlete **BO JACKSON** was doing his thing. Jackson won the 1985 Heisman Trophy at Auburn, but was also a standout baseball player. He signed with the Kansas City Royals and reached the Major Leagues in 1986. The Los Angeles Raiders picked him in the 1987 NFL Draft anyway. Jackson was able to play part-time for the Raiders after his Royals season was over.

Jackson thrilled NFL fans with his breakaway speed, repeatedly outracing defensive backs on long runs. As a baseball player, he was a powerful home run hitter. His speed helped him chase down balls in the outfield. An ad campaign "showed" him playing lots of other sports as well. A hip injury ended his football career in 1990, and he played in the Majors until 1994.

SUPER STAT

SIZE OF PERRY'S SUPER BOWL XX RING, THE LARGEST EVER AND MORE THAN TWICE THE SIZE OF THE AVERAGE MALE RING

Who was known as "The Fridge"?

Being big was nothing new for **WILLIAM "REFRIGERATOR" PERRY**. The future superstar weighed 200 pounds as an 11-year-old, and was extremely athletic for his size. Perry got his nickname at Clemson University. Teammate Ray Brown once got into the elevator with Perry. There was barely any room for the two of them, so Brown said, "Man, you're about as big as a refrigerator." With that comment, a legend was born.

The Chicago Bears drafted Perry as a defender, but used him in short-yardage situations, too. He would block for Walter Payton, or bulldoze into the line himself for a first down or score. In Super Bowl XX, Perry scored on a 1-yard run in Chicago's 46–10 win.

FAST FACT: Workouts with his father, Archie, helped Donald develop into a tackling machine. They lifted weights in a basement gym they called "The Dungeon" in their Pittsburgh home.

DID YOU KNOW?

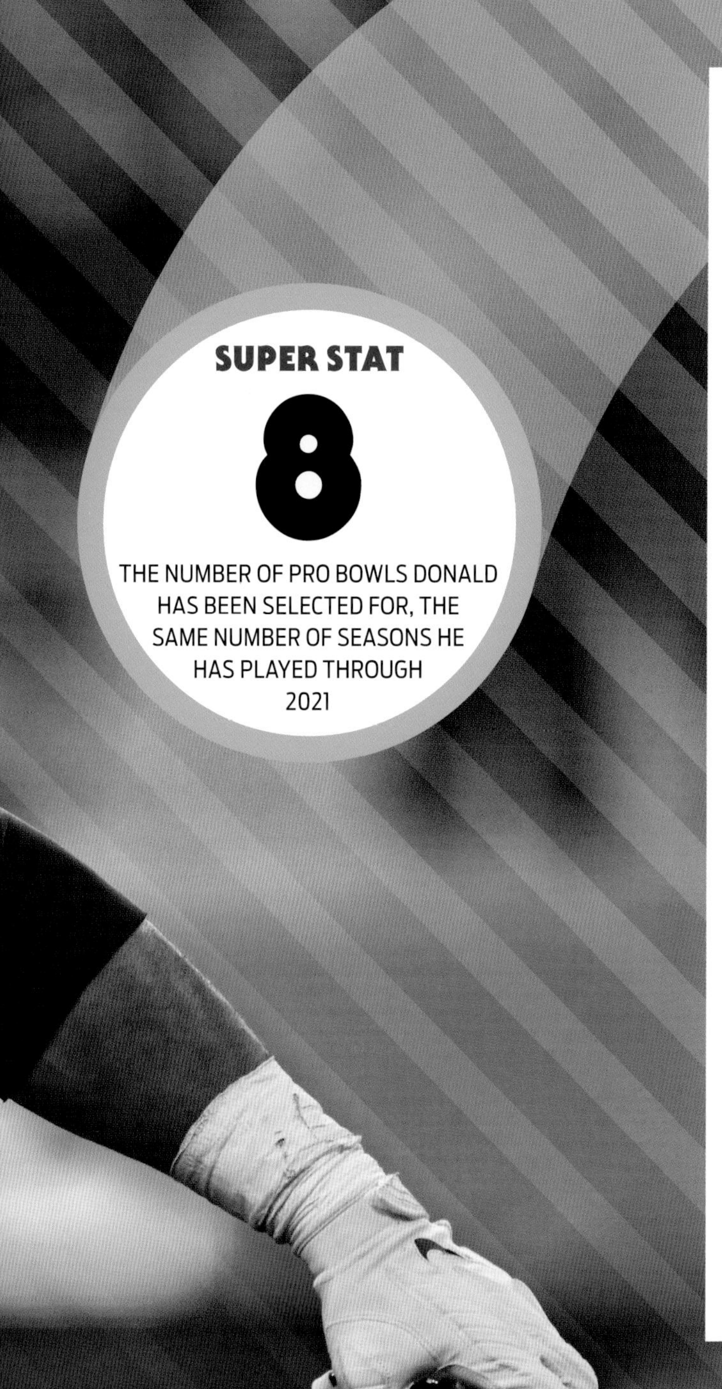

SUPER STAT

8

THE NUMBER OF PRO BOWLS DONALD HAS BEEN SELECTED FOR, THE SAME NUMBER OF SEASONS HE HAS PLAYED THROUGH 2021

What Rams sack machine has won three NFL Defensive Player of the Year Awards?

Few current NFL players are clearly among the league's all-time greats. One player easily makes that list: **AARON DONALD**. From his first season in 2014 when he was named the AP Defensive Rookie of the Year, Donald has been mauling opposing offenses, especially quarterbacks. Even though he plays defensive tackle, he reaches the passer regularly, racking up 10 or more sacks in six seasons, including an NFL-best 20.5 in 2018, when he won his second Defensive Player of the Year award; he won it for the first time in 2017. He became only the third player to win that honor three times when he won in 2020. While Donald has piled up individual honors—as well as one of the NFL's biggest contracts for a defensive player—the biggest prize eluded him until the 2021 season. Led by Donald on defense and Matthew Stafford on offense, the Los Angeles Rams won the Super Bowl for the first time.

Aaron Donald and the Rams took their Super Bowl LIII loss to the New England Patriots hard. Donald was especially disappointed and vowed to earn a ring if he got another chance. When the 2021 Rams made it to the Super Bowl against the Cincinnati Bengals, Donald was ready. Even though the Cincinnati offense focused on stopping him, he had two sacks, two tackles for loss, and four total tackles. His biggest play came at the end when he forced Joe Burrow to throw a fourth-down incompletion that sealed the Rams' win. It was time to celebrate!

Players whose feats set the standards by which future accomplishments are measured

RECORD B

REAKERS

FAST FACT: McCaffrey's best game during his super 2019 season came in a 34–27 win over Jacksonville. He ran for 176 yards, scoring twice, while catching six passes for 61 yards and another score.

SUPER STAT

14

THE SINGLE-GAME HIGH IN RECEPTIONS FOR MCCAFFREY DURING HIS RECORD-SETTING 2018 SEASON

Who holds the record for most single-season catches by a running back?

With his ninth catch in a 2018 game against the Atlanta Falcons, Carolina Panthers running back **CHRISTIAN McCAFFREY** topped a mark set by the Chicago Bears' Matt Forte. McCaffrey's 103 catches to that point (he finished with 107) were the most ever by a running back. That also became a new Panthers' single-season record for all players. All-around skills were nothing new to this former Stanford All-American. The first-round pick of the Panthers in 2017, McCaffrey had 80 catches as a rookie. In 2018, he also had 1,098 rushing yards to go along with his record number of catches. But his best season was 2019, when he ran for 1,387 yards while catching 116 passes for 1,005 yards. The catches, of course, extended his NFL record, but he also became only the third player ever with 1,000 yards both rushing and receiving. His 2,392 yards from scrimmage led the league, of course, but was also the third-highest total of all-time. He also scored 19 total touchdowns.

Catching footballs flying through the air is a McCaffrey family tradition. Christian's father, Ed, played 13 NFL seasons with the Giants, 49ers, and Broncos. Christian's 107 catches in 2018 topped Ed's career-best of 101, which he set in 2000 with Denver. However, the son still has a ways to go to catch the father in one area. "He's got three Super Bowl [rings]," Christian said. "So he's got me there." After playing at Stanford like his son, Ed McCaffrey won Super Bowls with San Francisco (XXIX) and Denver (XXXII and XXXIII).

Who has returned the most kicks for scores?

When it comes to returning kickoffs and punts, **DEVIN HESTER** is the greatest in NFL history. While playing for the Chicago Bears on December 20, 2010, Hester broke the all-time record for most career return touchdowns. His 64-yard punt return was his 14th return TD in a regular-season game. That season, he also led the league in punt return touchdowns (3). Through the 2016 season, Hester had 20 career non-offensive touchdowns, the most in NFL history. He is also the all-time leader in punt return TDs (14).

Who set a record in 2020 with nine games of at least one passing and one rushing TD?

In 2020, the multitalented young quarterback **KYLER MURRAY** of the Arizona Cardinals showed just how "multi" he is. Murray ran for at least one touchdown in each of his team's first nine games that season. He also had at least one TD pass in all of those games. He became the first ever with an eight-for-nine streak like that. In November, he set a single-season record with his ninth such game. Murray continued his success in 2021, becoming the first player to reach 70 career TD passes and 20 TD runs in his first three NFL seasons.

SUPER STAT

8

NUMBER OF CAREER TOUCHDOWNS FITZGERALD HAS SCORED IN THE PRO BOWL, WHICH IS MORE THAN ANY OTHER PLAYER

Who has the most receiving yards in one post-season?

It didn't take **LARRY FITZGERALD** long to become an NFL superstar. He led the league with 103 receptions in 2005 in only his second season. He was selected to play in the Pro Bowl seven times in his first nine seasons.

Fitzgerald's biggest accomplishment came in early 2009, after he helped lead the Arizona Cardinals to the playoffs for the first time in 10 years. Fitzgerald set records for most receiving yards and most touchdowns by a wide receiver in a single post-season. He caught 30 passes for 546 yards and seven touchdowns in only four games! Although the Cardinals fell short of winning the Super Bowl when they lost to the Pittsburgh Steelers, 27–23, Fitzgerald's performance is one that Arizona fans will surely never forget.

FAST FACT: T.J. Watt's total of 22.5 sacks in 2021 raises a question: How do you get half a sack? If two players work together to bring down a quarterback, each is credited with 0.5 sacks.

DID YOU KNOW?

SUPER STAT

21

NUMBER OF TACKLES FOR LOSS BY T.J. WATT IN 2021, THE SECOND YEAR IN A ROW HE LED THE NFL IN THAT STAT CATEGORY

Who tied the single-season record for sacks in 2021?

Pittsburgh Steelers linebacker/edge rusher **T.J. WATT** knew the path to the quarterback. Power forward at the snap, then attack! He had led the league with 15 sacks in 2020, but reached new heights in 2021, when he tied New York Giants' Hall of Famer **MICHAEL STRAHAN** for the NFL record of 22.5 sacks in a season. He had topped his 2020 mark in the season's next-to-last game with four sacks. On the final Sunday, Watt took down Tyler Huntley of the Baltimore Ravens for the record-tying tackle. And he reached the mark while missing two games earlier in the season with minor injuries.

While Watt knew the way to the QB, making his way to the NFL took a little more work. Growing up in a football family (see "Did You Know?"), Watt always had his eyes on the big prize. Like older brother J.J., T.J. attended Wisconsin. However, due to some knee problems, he was struggling with his play. Supported by his family, though, he battled back. In the summer before his junior year, he worked out every day. He learned from J.J. about the need for the right nutrition. And he had a standout junior season. T.J. was a starter from the moment he joined Pittsburgh in 2017 and earned his first Pro Bowl selection a year later. In 2021, he was the Defensive Player of the Year.

Backyard football games at the Watt family home were probably worth putting on TV. While T.J. Watt made headlines in 2021 with his record-tying sack total, older brother J.J. was already a three-time Defensive Player of the Year with the Houston Texans. and a two-time sacks leader. He joined the Arizona Cardinals in 2021. Derek Watt had joined the NFL as a fullback in 2016. By 2020, he was T.J.'s teammate on the Steelers. The brothers started out as hockey standouts before switching full-time to football in high school.

Who was named NFC Defensive Player of the Month a record three times in one season?

As a defensive back with the Green Bay Packers, **CHARLES WOODSON** earned a record three out of four NFC Defensive Player of the Month honors on his way to winning the 2009 NFL Defensive Player of the Year award. He led the league with nine interceptions and three touchdowns on interception returns.

Woodson had been a star since his college days at the University of Michigan. As a junior in 1997, he became the only defensive player to ever win the Heisman Trophy, the award given to college football's most outstanding player. Woodson had eight interceptions during the 1997 season. He also had a famous touchdown on a punt return against rival Ohio State to help lead Michigan to an undefeated season and share of the national title.

SUPER STAT

11

NUMBER OF CAREER INTERCEPTIONS CHARLES WOODSON RETURNED FOR TOUCHDOWNS, TIED FOR SECOND ALL-TIME

Who has the record for most completions by a rookie?

When **JUSTIN HERBERT** showed up for work on the second Sunday of his rookie season in 2020 with the Los Angeles Chargers, he was ready to wait his turn. He had his clipboard and his baseball cap, ready to watch Tyrod Taylor lead the Chargers. But during the kickoff, coach Anthony Lynn called for Herbert and told him he was starting the game. Taylor had had a bad reaction to a painkilling shot and could not play. The sixth-overall draft pick was ready. Herbert threw for 311 yards. Though the Chargers lost the first four games with Herbert in charge, Lynn left him in there. By the end of the season, Herbert had completed 396 passes, by far the most ever by a rookie quarterback. From Week 4 to Week 10, he had at least two TD passes in each of the seven games, the first rookie ever to do that, too. He was named the Offensive Rookie of the Year. In 2021, he topped all of his previous totals and earned his first Pro Bowl spot.

FAST FACT: Derrick Thomas was voted to the Pro Bowl in each of his first nine NFL seasons.

Who has the record for most sacks in one game?

SUPER STAT

20

NUMBER OF SACKS THOMAS RECORDED IN 1990; HE'S ONE OF ONLY TWELVE PLAYERS TO REACH THAT MANY SACKS IN ONE SEASON

Most of the 1970s and all of the '80s were a difficult time to be a fan of the Kansas City Chiefs: The team reached the NFL playoffs only once between 1972 and '89. It was no coincidence that the team's fortunes began to change soon after the arrival of linebacker **DERRICK THOMAS**.

Opposing NFL offenses took notice when Thomas was selected by the Chiefs with the fourth overall pick of the 1989 NFL Draft. It didn't take him long to emerge as an elite pass-rusher, at which point those same offenses began to dread playing against Kansas City. Thomas averaged nearly 12 sacks per season throughout the 1990s, and his stellar play was the foundation of a defensive unit that twice ranked as the NFL's best during that time. The Chiefs' defense was the key to Kansas City reaching the playoffs seven times that decade.

The best game of Thomas's Hall of Fame career came against the Seattle Seahawks on November 11, 1990. That day, Thomas sacked Seattle quarterback Dave Krieg seven times to break the single-game record of six set by San Francisco's Fred Dean in 1983. Krieg managed to avoid yet another sack on the game's final play, when he dodged Thomas before throwing a touchdown pass for a 17–16 win.

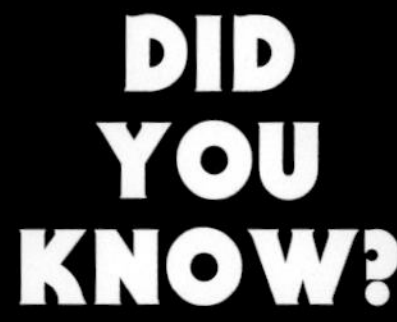

Three players have come within one sack of Derrick Thomas's record seven-sack effort in 1990. Fred Dean of San Francisco (1983); Osi Umeniyora of the New York Giants (2007); and Adrian Clayborn of the Falcons (2017). Thomas himself also had a six-sack game in 1998.

Who has the most receptions in a season?

As the NFL has become a league much more focused on passing and receiving in recent years, the record for most catches by a single player has gone up and up. The latest to set the all-time mark is **MICHAEL THOMAS** of the New Orleans Saints, who caught 149 passes in 2019. Detroit's Herman Moore had 123 catches in 1995, but since then seven players have topped him. At least one player has topped 123 grabs in all but two seasons since 2014. Thomas himself had 125 catches the year before he set the new record. Cooper Kupp of the Los Angeles Rams almost overtook Thomas in 2021, falling four catches short of tying him. On his way to the record in 2019, Thomas had nine games with at least 10 catches, including a season-high 13 in a loss to the Falcons. He also led the NFL that year with 1,725 receiving yards and was named the Offensive Player of the Year.

SUPER STAT

32

NUMBER OF CAREER TOUCHDOWN PASSES THOMAS HAD CAUGHT THROUGH THE 2021 NFL SEASON

SUPER STAT

12

JACKSON'S NUMBER OF GAMES WITH 100 OR MORE RUSHING YARDS, THE MOST BY AN NFL QUARTERBACK FOR A CAREER

Who is the youngest quarterback to start a playoff game?

Baltimore Ravens QB **LAMAR JACKSON** was one day short of his 22nd birthday when he led his team onto the field for a Wild-Card Playoff Game in January 2019. The Heisman Trophy winner at Louisville, Jackson had taken over as the Ravens' starter with seven games left in the regular season. He quickly led them to six wins in those seven games. while showing off the passing and running talents that would soon make him an NFL MVP in 2019. But for the moment, he had to deal with the Chargers and the question of his age. "I'm here to play football. I was 21 all year, so this is another game for me," Jackson said. Jackson threw two late TD passes, but the Ravens lost to the Chargers 23–17. That rookie season set the stage for a spectacular 2019, when Jackson led the NFL with 36 TD passes, while rushing for 1,206 yards and seven more scores.

Who holds the records for most post-season sacks in a career and in one game?

Linebacker **WILLIE McGINEST** was a key force on three Super Bowl–winning teams for the New England Patriots. He also played defensive end, and he seemed to save his best performances for the biggest games. In 18 career playoff contests, McGinest racked up a record 16 sacks. He set a single-game postseason record during the final playoff run of his career, with 4½ sacks in a 28–3 blowout of the Jacksonville Jaguars in a January 2006 playoff game.

FAST FACT: Despite being the NFL's all-time leader in career sacks, Bruce Smith never led the league in any one season. He did finish second in sacks three times, in 1990, '93, and '96.

Who has the most career sacks?

Although NFL offensive linemen constantly double- and triple-teamed **BRUCE SMITH**, the Buffalo Bills defensive end recorded 10 or more sacks in a season 13 times. Smith is the NFL's all-time leader with 200 career sacks. He was selected to play in the Pro Bowl 11 times, and he was a key player on Buffalo teams that reached four straight Super Bowls in the early 1990s.

Smith had an elite combination of speed and size. He could outflank blockers, spin inside of them, or simply bulldoze right through them. One of Smith's hardest hits knocked New York Jets quarterback Boomer Esiason out for four games. Still, Esiason said, "If I was a football coach and had Bruce Smith as my player, I would say to [young players], 'This is how you have to be.'"

Who had the most yards by a tight end in his first three seasons?

As a fifth-round selection by San Francisco in the 2017 NFL Draft, **GEORGE KITTLE** was not expected to dominate. And as a rookie, he was true to form, catching 43 passes for a respectable 515 yards. But in 2018, he blew way past expectations, grabbing 88 catches for an incredible 1,377 yards, one of the highest totals ever for a tight end. When he had another great year in 2019 (1,053 yards on 85 grabs), he put his name in the record books. His total of 2,945 receiving yards are the most ever by a tight end in his first three seasons.

SUPER STAT

1,416

SINGLE-SEASON RECEIVING YARDS RECORD FOR A TIGHT END, SET BY KANSAS CITY'S TRAVIS KELCE IN 2020

SUPER STAT

75

NUMBER OF CAREER TOUCHDOWN CATCHES BY EVANS, TIED FOR FOURTH-MOST ALL-TIME AMONG ACTIVE PLAYERS

Who began his career with an NFL-record eight seasons with 1,000 receiving yards?

A lot has changed in the NFL since the 2014 season. New champions have emerged, new rules have altered the game, and some all-time stars have retired. But one thing has been the same, year after year. **MIKE EVANS** has ended every season with at least 1,000 receiving yards for the Tampa Bay Buccaneers. That streak of eight is the most ever by a player in his first eight seasons. It's also a streak that is third-best all-time, topped only by Jerry Rice with 10 and Tim Brown with nine. Three other players have eight, like Evans. Only Randy Moss, with six such seasons from the start of a career, can challenge Evans. The former Texas A&M star was the seventh-overall pick by the Bucs. He had a great rookie year, racking up 1,051 yards to get his streak started. He also had 12 TD catches for the first of four career years with 12 or more. He had his best season in 2016, with career bests of 96 catches and 1,321 yards, to go along with another dozen TD catches. In 2020, Evans and the Bucs welcomed Tom Brady, who aimed enough passes at Evans for the receiver to set new career highs in TD catches two years in a row.

DID YOU KNOW

FAST FACT: In 2021, Evans had 14 touchdown catches, setting a new Tampa Bay record. The old record? Set by a guy named Mike Evans, who had 13 in 2020!

Tampa Bay Buccaneers fans were excited when all-time superstar Tom Brady joined their team in 2020. But they were not nearly as happy as Evans. His excited video praising Brady was seen by millions. "That's Tom Brady, bro. . . ," said Evans. "The greatest of all-time. He's a franchise changer . . . and he understands the game of football like nobody else understands that level besides the greats. It's going to be great to work with him." Evans was right. Brady was a franchise changer, working with Evans to lead the Bucs to a Super Bowl championship in their first season together.

SUPER STAT

2

NUMBER OF WOMEN'S WORLD CUP SOCCER CHAMPIONSHIPS WON BY JULIE ERTZ, ZACH'S WIFE

Who has the record for most receptions by a tight end in one season?

Most of the important tight end receiving records have been set in the past decade or so. The position has taken on a bigger role in many teams' passing offenses. **TRAVIS KELCE** set the single-season receiving record (page 69). Rob Gronkowski's single-season TD mark came in 2011 (page 85). And George Kittle is in the record books for his three-season receiving record (page 69). In 2018, **ZACH ERTZ** of the Philadelphia Eagles joined in the fun. With his tenth catch in a big late-season win over the Houston Texans, Ertz passed the previous record, which was set in 2010 by Dallas's Jason Witten, with 110 receptions. Ertz ended that 2018 season with 116 receptions, a new all-time best for tight ends. He also had a career-best 1,163 receiving yards, and his eight touchdown catches tied his single-season best as well.

Who has the most receptions in one game?

If you asked an NFL coach to design the perfect possession receiver, his image would likely resemble **BRANDON MARSHALL**. A quick 6´5˝ wideout with the strength of a lineman, Marshall's aggressive after-the-catch running made him the perfect target on short passes.

In Week 14 of the 2009 season, the Denver Broncos' offensive game plan was simple: Quarterback Kyle Orton throws to Marshall. Of the 28 passes Orton tossed his way, Marshall caught a record 21 of them for 200 yards. In response to the Indianapolis Colts' defensive scheme, Orton said, "You give me that matchup, and I'll take it 100 times out of 100 times." All told, Marshall accounted for more than half of his team's yards that day.

SUPER STAT

4

THE NUMBER OF TOUCHDOWNS MARSHALL SCORED IN THE PRO BOWL IN JANUARY 2012, WHICH SET A NEW RECORD

SUPER STAT

75

NUMBER OF YARDS ON THE LONGEST SUPER BOWL TOUCHDOWN RUN, SET BY PITTSBURGH'S WILLIE PARKER IN SUPER BOWL XL

Who caught the longest TD pass in Super Bowl history?

Both of the key players on this play would probably trade their spot in the record book for a Super Bowl ring, but at least they set a record in defeat. In Super Bowl XXXVIII, the Carolina Panthers took on the New England Patriots. The Tom Brady-led Pats were ahead 21–16 in the fourth quarter. But Carolina picked off a Brady pass and took over at their own 10-yard line. After two incompletions and a New England penalty, Carolina QB Jake Delhomme saw wide receiver **MUHSIN MUHAMMAD** streaking up the left sideline. Delhomme heaved a 50-yard rainbow that Muhammad caught past mid-field. He sprinted the rest of the way. The TD gave Carolina a 22-21 lead and at 85 yards was the longest offensive touchdown ever scored in a Super Bowl. The play turned out to be the longest in either the QB's or the receiver's career. Unfortunately for the Panthers, Brady ended up leading the Patriots to a final-play field goal to win the game.

FAST FACT: Forced fumbles didn't become an official stat until 1991. Former defensive end Robert Mathis holds the career record with 54, two ahead of Julius Peppers.

Who has the record for most forced fumbles in one game?

Chicago Bears cornerback **CHARLES TILLMAN** mastered the art of separating the football from offensive players. He did so by using a perfectly timed swipe of his fist, a move that became known as the "Peanut Punch." "My aunt gave me the nickname when I was a little baby, and it just stuck," Tillman says of why he's called "Peanut." "I was a small kid growing up."

Tillman set an NFL record for most forced fumbles in a game, with four in a 51–20 win over the Tennessee Titans in 2012. "Peanut" finished the season with 10 forced fumbles, which tied an NFL record.

Who was the first to win three NFL Defensive Player of the Year awards?

The great New York Giants linebacker **LAWRENCE TAYLOR** changed the NFL forever when he came into the league as a rookie in 1981. The linebacker terrorized opposing quarterbacks and was named NFL Defensive Player of the Year, an award he won again in 1982 and 1986, the first player to win three of those awards in one career. Since then, **J.J. WATT** (2012, 2014, 2015) and Aaron Donald (2017, 2018, 2020) have matched the great LT in award totals. They'll never match him in his impact on the game.

DID YOU KNOW?

SUPER STAT

4

THE NUMBER OF SEASONS THAT ERIC DICKERSON LED THE NFL IN RUSHING (1983, 1984, 1986, 1988)

Who holds the record for most rushing yards in a single season?

For some famous stats, all you need to say is the number and fans know what you're talking about. In the NFL, one of those numbers is 2,105. That's how many rushing yards **ERIC DICKERSON** of the Los Angeles Rams piled up in 1984. On the way to the record that season, Dickerson had 10 games with at least 120 yards rushing. His best games were 215 yards against the Houston Oilers and 208 yards against the St. Louis Cardinals. (Yes, those were real NFL teams; look 'em up!) Dickerson broke the record in that game against Houston, topping the old mark of 2,003 set by O.J. Simpson in 1973. Incredibly, Dickerson was not named the MVP that season, finishing second in the voting to **DAN MARINO**, who set a new single-season record of his own with 48 TD passes. Dickerson led the NFL in rushing three other times and was named to six Pro Bowls. He was inducted into the Pro Football Hall of Fame in 1999.

FAST FACT: Dickerson was well-known for his upright, speedy running style. He was also known for the clear plastic goggles that he wore most of his career. He needed them for vision, since contact lenses popped out when he was hit during games.

Wait, there's more! Dickerson certainly earned his spot in the all-time record books for his still-unmatched 1984 season. But setting records was nothing new for him. In 1983, his rookie season, he ran for 1,808 yards, a new all-time best for a player in his first season. That broke a record set in 1981 by George Rogers of the New Orleans Saints with 1,674 yards. And no rookie player since Dickerson has come closer than Dallas's Ezekiel Elliott in 2016, when he had 1,631 rushing yards.

SUPER S

Their specialty is putting the ball either through the uprights or into the end zone

CORERS

FAST FACT: Newton wore the Number 2 on his uniform at Auburn. He switched to Number 1 because another player, quarterback Jimmy Clausen, wore Number 2 for the Panthers when Newton was drafted by Carolina.

SUPER STAT

62

COMBINED PASSING AND RUSHING TOUCHDOWNS CAM NEWTON SCORED IN HIS FIRST TWO SEASONS

DID YOU KNOW?

Who has the most rushing touchdowns by a quarterback in one season?

A lot was expected of **CAM NEWTON** when the Carolina Panthers selected the 6'5" quarterback with the first overall pick of the 2011 NFL Draft. Yet Newton still managed to exceed those high expectations with one of the most productive seasons ever for a rookie quarterback. He did it with both his arm and his legs. Newton became the first rookie in NFL history to throw for 4,000 passing yards, and he also scored 14 rushing touchdowns. It was the most rushing touchdowns ever by a quarterback in one season, breaking the record of 12 set by the New England Patriots' Steve Grogan in 1976.

Newton wasted no time making an impact in the NFL. In his first pro game, against the Arizona Cardinals, he threw for 422 yards. The following week, he threw for 432 yards against the Green Bay Packers. He became the first quarterback—rookie or not—to throw for as many as 854 yards through the first two games of an NFL season. After another great season in 2012, Newton became the first player to reach both 40 passing TDs and 20 rushing TDs in just two NFL seasons.

The big Panther was not done. In 2015, he was named the NFL MVP after throwing 35 touchdown passes and running for another 10 TDs. Carolina had a 15–1 record. In the NFC Championship Game, Newton ran for two scores and passed for two more. That win carried the Panthers to Super Bowl 50, where they lost to the Denver Broncos. Newton played for Carolina through 2019. After a season in New England in 2020, he returned to the Panthers for the 2021 season.

Not only did Cam Newton win the 2010 Heisman Trophy as college football's top player, but he also led his Auburn University Tigers to that season's national championship. He joined Tony Dorsett and Charles Woodson as winners of the Heisman, a national championship, and the NFL Rookie of the Year award.

Heisman Trophy

BCS National Championship

NFL Rookie of the Year award

Who threw the most TD passes in one Super Bowl quarter?

Washington quarterback **DOUG WILLIAMS** put Super Bowl XXII out of reach of the Denver Broncos with a record-setting four-touchdown performance in the second quarter. Williams's team went on to win 42–10 and he was named the game's MVP. Williams also made history that day as the first Black starting quarterback to win a Super Bowl trophy. After a career with Tampa Bay and Washington, Williams became a college football coach and later a key member of the Washington front office.

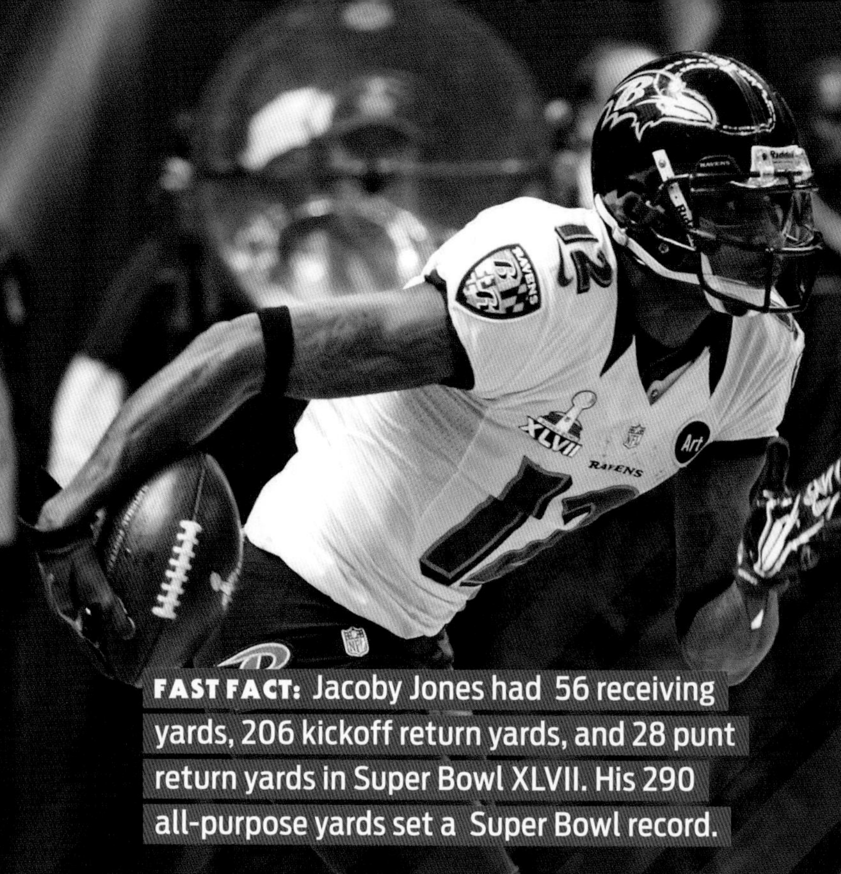

FAST FACT: Jacoby Jones had 56 receiving yards, 206 kickoff return yards, and 28 punt return yards in Super Bowl XLVII. His 290 all-purpose yards set a Super Bowl record.

Who has scored the longest touchdown in a Super Bowl?

Baltimore Ravens wide receiver and return specialist **JACOBY JONES** received the opening kickoff of the second half of Super Bowl XLVII eight yards deep in his own end zone. Many players would have taken a knee for a touchback. Jones, however, raced up the middle of the field and barely had to break stride as he went 108 yards to the end zone. It was the longest play of any kind in Super Bowl history.

Jones's record-breaking return was his second long touchdown of the game. With less than two minutes to go before halftime, he fell down to haul in a long pass. Because he was untouched on the play, he scrambled to his feet before juking two San Francisco 49ers and finishing off a 56-yard score.

SUPER STAT

5

NUMBER OF RUSHING TOUCHDOWNS SEATTLE'S SHAUN ALEXANDER SCORED IN A 2002 GAME TO SET THE NFL RECORD FOR A HALF

Who is the only player to rush for three touchdowns of more than 40 yards in the same game?

Many running backs have scored two long touchdown runs in one game. But only **DOUG MARTIN** of the Tampa Bay Buccaneers once scored on *three* runs of at least 40 yards in a single contest. He did it on scampers of 45, 67, and 70 yards in a 42–32 win over the Oakland Raiders on November 4, 2012, and he did so while rushing for 251 yards. He joined former Denver Broncos running back Mike Anderson as the only NFL players to run for more than 250 yards and four scores in one game. Martin's performance helped earn him an invitation to the Pro Bowl after an oustanding rookie season.

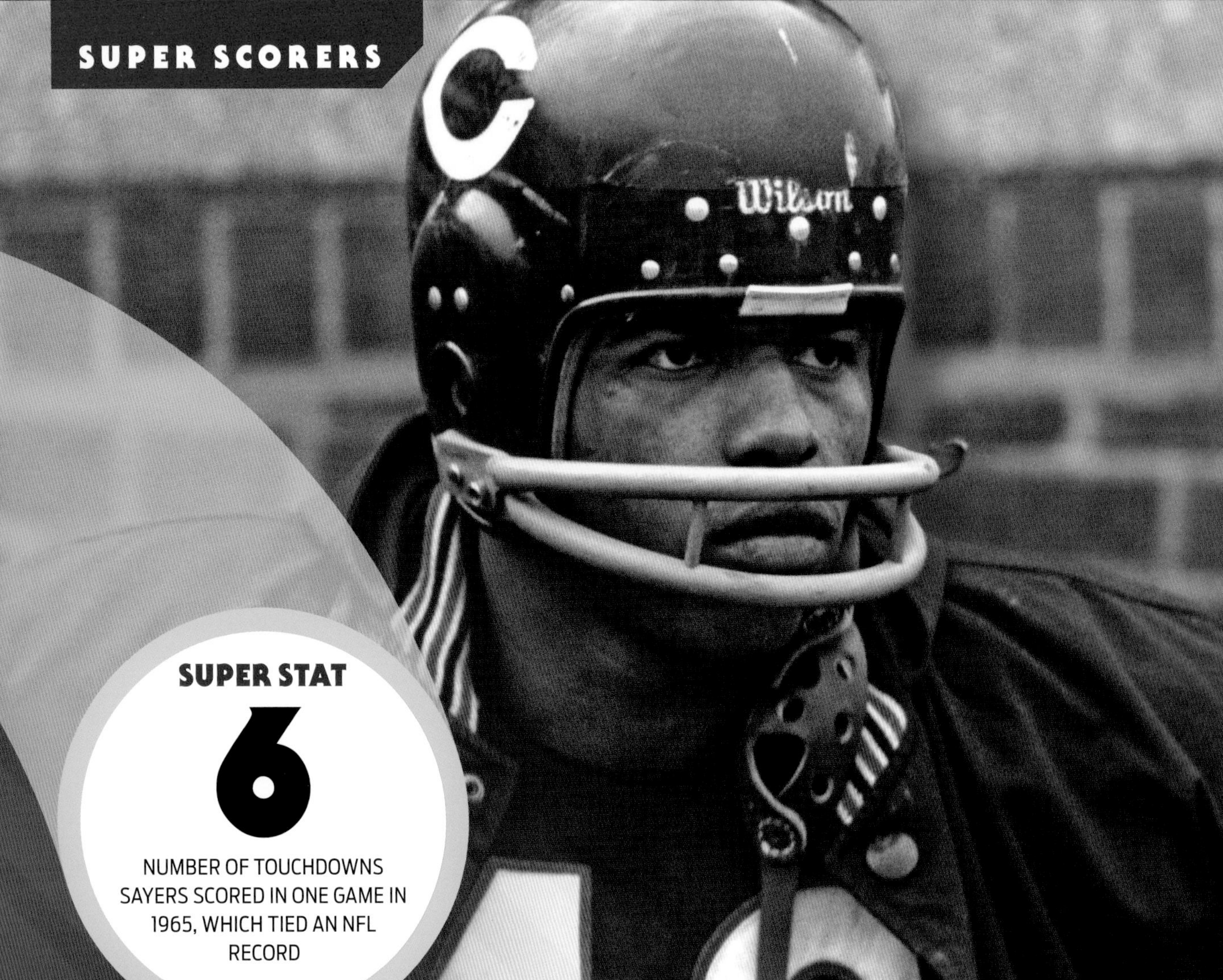

SUPER STAT

6

NUMBER OF TOUCHDOWNS SAYERS SCORED IN ONE GAME IN 1965, WHICH TIED AN NFL RECORD

Who has the record for most touchdowns by a rookie?

Hall of Fame running back **GALE SAYERS** scored 22 touchdowns during his rookie season with the Chicago Bears, in 1965. Known as the "Kansas Comet" because of the blazing speed he showed at the University of Kansas, Sayers was a hot prospect coming out of college. Both the Bears of the NFL and the Kansas City Chiefs, who were then part of the American Football League, selected him in the first round of their leagues' 1965 drafts.

Sayers also holds the career record for kickoff return average, with 30.6 yards per return. An injury to his right knee, and then one to his left knee two years later, limited his career to just 68 NFL games from 1965 to '71. Like a comet, he burned brilliantly for a short time.

Who has the most touchdowns by a tight end in one season?

The 18 touchdown catches **ROB GRONKOWSKI** had for the New England Patriots in 2011 are the most ever for a tight end in one season.

What the man known as "Gronk" has become most famous for, however, is his extremely hard spiking of the ball to celebrate a touchdown. "The Gronk Spike," as it has become known, debuted during the third game of the tight end's rookie season, in 2010. Gronkowski kicks up his left knee, hops a few times on his right leg, and slams the ball into the ground. After nine seasons in New England, Gronk joined Tampa Bay in 2020.

SUPER STAT

60

ESTIMATED SPEED IN MILES PER HOUR THAT GRONKOWSKI SPIKES THE BALL IN HIS TOUCHDOWN CELEBRATION

FAST FACT: In 2007, Jason Taylor won the Walter Payton Man of the Year Award for his off-the-field charitable work.

SUPER STAT

9

NUMBER OF DEFENSIVE TOUCHDOWNS TAYLOR SCORED, MOST EVER BY A DEFENSIVE LINEMAN

Who has the most career touchdowns on fumble returns?

Throughout his 15-year NFL career, **JASON TAYLOR** was known as a disruptive force who consistently made game-changing plays on the defensive side of the ball. He was constantly around the action, whether dropping running backs behind the line of scrimmage or pulling down quarterbacks in the pocket. It was his relentless pursuit of the football that enabled Taylor to score six career touchdowns on fumble returns, which is the most in NFL history.

Taylor's best season was 2006, when he was named NFL Defensive Player of the Year as a defensive end for the Miami Dolphins. Not only did he set a career-high with nine forced fumbles, but he tied for the NFL lead with two touchdowns on interception returns. That's a remarkable achievement, considering it's a category almost always led by defensive backs. Taylor was inducted into the Pro Football Hall of Fame in 2017.

DID YOU KNOW?

Jason Taylor showed off his moves during a 2008 TV stint on *Dancing with the Stars*. He and his partner, ballroom dancer Edyta Sliwinska, finished in second place among the competition's 12 pairs. They were topped only by former Olympic figure skating gold medalist Kristi Yamaguchi and ballroom dancer Mark Ballas.

SUPER STAT

7

RECORD-TYING NUMBER OF TD PASSES BLANDA THREW IN A GAME AGAINST THE NEW YORK TITANS IN 1961

Who is the oldest player to throw a touchdown?

On December 14, 1974, **GEORGE BLANDA** of the Oakland Raiders threw a 28-yard touchdown pass to wideout Cliff Branch in a game against the Dallas Cowboys. Since Blanda was born on September 17, 1927, that means he was 47 years, two months, and 27 days old when he threw what would turn out to be the final scoring pass of his NFL career.

Blanda's touchdown to Branch was the only pass he completed in 1974. He was the Raiders' kicker that season, and also a backup to starting quarterback Ken Stabler. Blanda's first NFL season had been 25 years earlier, in 1949. His best season was 1961, when he led the AFL with 3,330 passing yards and 36 touchdowns.

SUPER STAT

71

NUMBER OF PASSES WOODSON INTERCEPTED IN HIS CAREER, WHICH RANKS THIRD IN NFL HISTORY

Who has the most TDs on interception returns?

Hall of Fame defensive back **ROD WOODSON** holds the NFL record for most career touchdowns on interception returns. The 1993 Defensive Player of the Year ran 12 picks back for scores during his 17-year career.

Woodson went to Super Bowls as a member of three teams: the Pittsburgh Steelers, Baltimore Ravens, and Oakland Raiders. After having spent the majority of his career at cornerback, Woodson moved to safety as a 34-year-old with the Ravens in 1999. He tied for the NFL lead that season in interceptions, with seven. The following season, he started all 16 games on a defense that led the Ravens to a Super Bowl victory. That defense is often named among the greatest defenses in NFL history.

Who holds the record for most field goals in one game?

On October 21, 2007, Tennessee Titans kicker **ROB BIRONAS** broke the record for field goals made in one game when he booted eight through the uprights against the Houston Texans. As it turned out, the Titans needed all eight of those kicks.

Tennessee starting quarterback Vince Young was sidelined that day. His backup, Kerry Collins, was having trouble leading the team to touchdowns once the Titans drove into Houston territory. Tennessee kept settling for field goal attempts. In the fourth quarter, the Texans scored 29 points and took the lead, 36–35, with 57 seconds left in regulation. But Collins moved the Titans into position for one last field goal. Bironas drilled a 29-yarder as time expired to give Tennessee a 38–36 win.

On the day, Bironas connected from 52, 25, 21, 30, 28, 43, and twice from 29 yards. The previous record of seven field goals in one game had been held by four different NFL kickers.

FAST FACT: The first placekicker to reach seven field goals in a game was Jim Bakken of the St. Louis Cardinals. He knocked that many through the uprights in a 28–14 win over the Pittsburgh Steelers in a 1967 game.

SUPER STAT

35

NFL-LEADING NUMBER OF FIELD GOALS BIRONAS MADE DURING THE 2007 REGULAR SEASON

DID YOU KNOW?

Abilene Christian University's Ove Johansson kicked the longest field goal ever—in either college or pro —when he connected from 69 yards away on October 16, 1976. The kick came with 2:13 remaining in the first quarter of Abilene Christian's 17–0 victory over East Texas State.

Who completed the longest touchdown pass in overtime of a playoff game?

The 2011 Denver Broncos were in last place in the AFC West with a 1–4 record when they made **TIM TEBOW** their starting quarterback over Kyle Orton. Tebow turned Denver's season around,leading the team to a division title. He did so more with his legs than his arm, finishing second among NFL quarterbacks in rushing yards.

It was Tebow's arm, however, that led Denver to a playoff win over the Pittsburgh Steelers. He threw for 316 yards, 80 of which came on a TD pass to Demaryius Thomas on the first play of overtime. It was the longest overtime TD pass in playoff history.

SUPER STAT

2

NUMBER OF BCS NATIONAL CHAMPIONSHIPS TEBOW WON AS THE STARTING QUARTERBACK FOR FLORIDA

FAST FACT: Justin Tucker holds another big field-goal record: His seven seasons with 30 or more three-pointers is the most ever for a career.

Who kicked the longest field goal?

When you are a looong way from the end zone, but you have the NFL's best kicker, you always have a chance. That's where the Baltimore Ravens were on September 26, 2021. They trailed Detroit 17–16 with three seconds left. Kicker **JUSTIN TUCKER** was sent on to make a miracle. Tucker got his spot set, Long snapper Nick Moore zipped the ball back to holder Sam Koch, who got the ball down quickly. Tucker took his steps, swung his strong leg and then watched. The ball flew and flew, end over end, and finally bounced on the crossbar! The ball twisted up and then over before finishing its path to history. The kick was good from 66 yards, the longest ever in NFL history, beating the old mark by two yards. Tucker then made it memorable with a field-long sprint holding up the ball, helmet off and screaming. Oh, yes, it also gave the Ravens a 19–17 win.

Who scored the most points in a Super Bowl game?

New England was down 28-3 late in the first half to the Atlanta Falcons in Super Bowl LI. That's when Patriots running back **JAMES WHITE** scored his team's first TD. He added a two-point conversion on a TD by Julian Edelman in the second half. Then White scored again to finally tie the game with less than a minute left. When he plunged into the end zone to score the first overtime TD in Super Bowl history, he and the Patriots had completed a record-setting comeback. White's 20 total points were a record, too.

FAST FACT: Rice developed his reliable hands when he was a kid—he caught bricks on a scaffold while he assisted his father, who worked as a mason. Rice's pay was reduced for any bricks he would drop.

SUPER STAT

215

THE SUPER BOWL-RECORD NUMBER OF RECEIVING YARDS RICE GAINED IN HIS MVP PERFORMANCE IN SUPER BOWL XXIII, IN JANUARY 1989

DID YOU KNOW?

Who has scored the most touchdowns in NFL history?

On the first *Monday Night Fotball* game of the 1994 season, **JERRY RICE** of the San Francisco 49ers had a chance to break former Cleveland Browns running back Jim Brown's all-time NFL record of 126 career touchdowns. Rice had ended the 1993 season with 124 career TDs, so he needed two touchdowns to tie Brown, and three to break the record. Three touchdowns was a lot to expect in a game against a Los Angeles Raiders team that had made the playoffs the previous year and had the NFL's fifth-best pass defense in 1993. The Raiders had also improved their secondary from the previous year by signing cornerback Albert Lewis away from the Kansas City Chiefs.

Rice wasted little time reaching the end zone, giving the 49ers a 7–0 lead in the first quarter with a 69-yard touchdown catch from quarterback Steve Young. Rice would not score again until the fourth quarter, when his TD on a 23-yard run tied Brown's record and gave San Francisco a 37–14 lead that put the game out of reach. The only suspense left was whether Rice would be able to set a new NFL career touchdown record in front of his home crowd and a national television audience.

Sure enough, Rice outleaped Lewis for a 38-yard touchdown late in the fourth quarter. It was his third touchdown of the game and the 127th of his career. He would go on to score an astounding 81 more times to finish with 208 touchdowns, which is 33 more than any other player and 51 more than any other receiver. Many consider Rice to be the best player in NFL history.

Jerry Rice played college football at a relatively small and obscure school called Mississippi Valley State University. It is a school that currently enrolls 2,500 students, which is more than the population of the city it's in, Itta Bena. MVSU is part of the Football Championship Subdivision (FCS), which was known as Division I-AA when Rice played there from 1981 to '84. The Jerry Rice Award now goes each season to the most outstanding freshman player in the FCS.

Who has scored the most touchdowns in one NFL season?

TD or LT? The San Diego Chargers' **LaDAINIAN TOMLINSON** went on a rampage in 2006. The most impressive mark he set that year was the single-season touchdown record. It was the fourth time in seven seasons that the record had been broken.

In 2000, Marshall Faulk of the St. Louis Rams scored 26 times to break the record of 25 that had been set by the Dallas Cowboys' Emmitt Smith. Three years later, Kansas City Chiefs running back Priest Holmes reached the end zone 27 times, and Shaun Alexander of the Seattle Seahawks scored 28 times two years after that. Tomlinson topped them all, and he didn't do it by just one touchdown. His superhuman effort landed him three ahead of Alexander, with 31 touchdowns on the season. He also led the league in rushing yards that year, and won the NFL MVP award.

SUPER STAT

38

NFL-RECORD NUMBER OF TIMES TOMLINSON RUSHED FOR TWO OR MORE TOUCHDOWNS IN ONE GAME

Who is the last player to score on a 99-yard touchdown reception?

In all, 13 NFL players have scored on the longest possible touchdown reception of 99 yards. The last one to do it was **VICTOR CRUZ** of the New York Giants, in a game against the New York Jets on Christmas Eve in 2011. Cruz caught a pass from quarterback Eli Manning 10 yards beyond the line of scrimmage. He avoided tackle attempts by Jets defensive backs Antonio Cromartie and Kyle Wilson before taking off down the right sideline, where he outran Jets safety Eric Smith to the end zone.

Cruz was signed by the Giants after going undrafted in 2010. His break came early in 2011, when injuries to Giants wideouts Mario Manningham and Domenik Hixon thrust Cruz into a bigger role. He responded by setting a team record for most receiving yards in a season with 1,536.

SUPER STAT

2

NUMBER OF 99-YARD TDS ON RUSHING PLAYS IN NFL HISTORY, BY TONY DORSETT IN 1993 AND DERRICK HENRY IN 2018

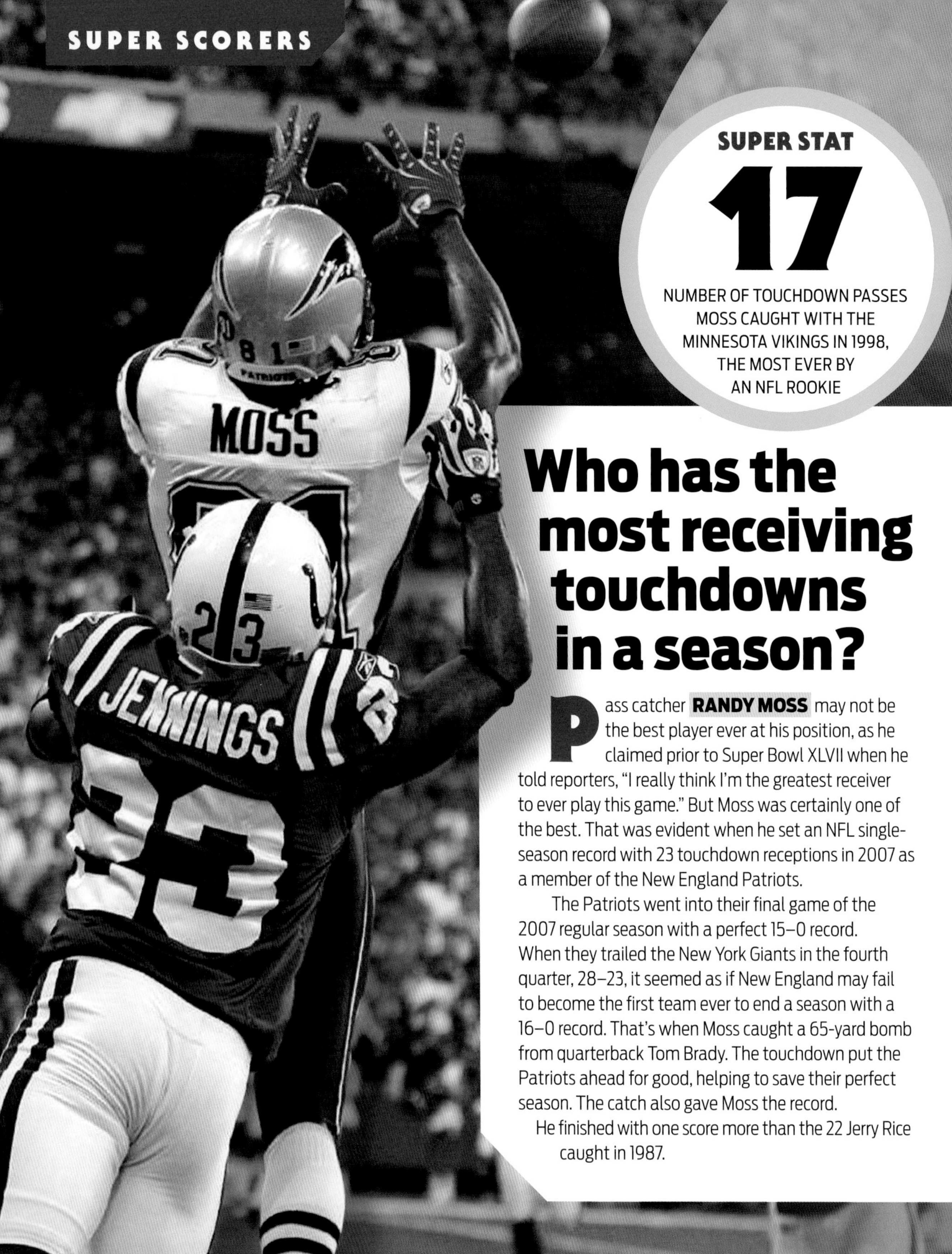

SUPER STAT

17

NUMBER OF TOUCHDOWN PASSES MOSS CAUGHT WITH THE MINNESOTA VIKINGS IN 1998, THE MOST EVER BY AN NFL ROOKIE

Who has the most receiving touchdowns in a season?

Pass catcher **RANDY MOSS** may not be the best player ever at his position, as he claimed prior to Super Bowl XLVII when he told reporters, "I really think I'm the greatest receiver to ever play this game." But Moss was certainly one of the best. That was evident when he set an NFL single-season record with 23 touchdown receptions in 2007 as a member of the New England Patriots.

The Patriots went into their final game of the 2007 regular season with a perfect 15–0 record. When they trailed the New York Giants in the fourth quarter, 28–23, it seemed as if New England may fail to become the first team ever to end a season with a 16–0 record. That's when Moss caught a 65-yard bomb from quarterback Tom Brady. The touchdown put the Patriots ahead for good, helping to save their perfect season. The catch also gave Moss the record. He finished with one score more than the 22 Jerry Rice caught in 1987.

FAST FACT: At age 23, Ben Roethlisberger became the youngest starting QB to win the Super Bowl.

Who holds the record for touchdown passes in consecutive games?

In the fall of 2014, **BEN ROETHLISBERGER** had a performance for the ages—and then repeated it again the following week. Big Ben is the first quarterback in NFL history to pass for six touchdowns in back-to-back games. In Week 8, he completed 40 of 49 attempts and passed for a career-high 522 yards and six touchdowns against the Indianapolis Colts. He tied for the third-most passing yards in a single game in NFL history. The following week, against the Baltimore Ravens, the 6'5" QB finished with 340 yards and another six TDs. Behind those big games, Roethlisberger finished the season tied for the league lead in passing yards (4,952). In 2021, after leading Pittsburgh to two Super Bowl titles and earning six Pro Bowl selections, Roethlisberger retired after a great 18-year career.

Who has the longest field goal by a rookie?

In their 2017 home game against the rival New York Giants, the Philadelphia Eagles sent rookie kicker **JAKE ELLIOTT** out to try a field goal to try to win it. Why not? The attempt was a longshot from 61 yards away, but the game was tied, so even if he missed, no harm. Instead, Elliott, who grew up and went to school in the Phily area, drilled the kick right through the uprights. The Eagles won 27–24 and Elliott's teammates carried him off in triumph. It was the longest field goal made by an NFL rookie. Elliott put himself in the record book again when the Eagles reached Super Bowl LII that season. His 46-yard field goal set a rookie record for the Super Bowl and capped his team's 41–33 win.

FAST FACT: Before Kupp won in 2021 and Michael Thomas won in 2019, the previous wide receiver to be named the AP Offensive Player of the Year was Jerry Rice, way back in 1993.

DID YOU KNOW?

Who was the last NFL player to win receiving's "Triple Crown"?

SUPER STAT

1

AFTER THE 2021 SEASON, KUPP'S PLACE ON THE RAMS' ALL-TIME SINGLE-SEASON RECORD LIST FOR RECEPTIONS AND RECEIVING YARDS

When his Los Angeles Rams team reached—and lost—Super Bowl LIII, star wide receiver **COOPER KUPP** could only sit and watch. An injury had knocked him out of the lineup. That disappointment after the 2018 season fueled the the start of an amazing run. In 2019, Kupp had 1,161 receiving yards and 10 TD catches. Injuries slowed him again in 2020, but in 2021, he put it all together. On the way to helping the Rams reach another Super Bowl—but this time, to win it—Kupp had one of the best seasons by a receiver in NFL history. He led the NFL with 145 catches and 1,947 receiving yards (both good for second-most in a season), as well as 16 touchdown receptions. He thus earned the "Triple Crown," a rare feat of leading the league in all the key receiving stats. The only other players to wear that mythical "crown" (since 1970) were Jerry Rice (1990), Sterling Sharpe (1992), and Steve Smith (2005). Kupp had five games with 10 or more catches, and seven games with 120 or more yards. In the postseason, he just kept things rolling. In three playoff games, he totaled 25 catches for four TDs. And he saved his biggest plays for the biggest games. He caught an 11-yard TD from Matthew Stafford to give the Rams a 13–3 lead over the Cincinnati Bengals in the Super Bowl. As the clock ran down and the Rams trailed, the pair connected again. Stafford zipped a 1-yard pass that Kupp leaped to snag for the winning points.

Setting records is nothing new for Cooper Kupp. After a solid high school career, he stayed near his hometown when he went to Eastern Washington University. He was not the biggest receiver around, but he ended up setting FCS career records with 428 catches, 73 for TDs, and 6,464 yards. He got some of his football talents from his family. Grandpa Jake was a 12-year NFL offensive lineman, while father Craig had a short NFL career as a quarterback. Even with all that, Kupp was only a third-round draft pick in 2017, proving that sometimes good things come to those who wait.

YARDAG

The players who have excelled at moving their teams up and down the field

E KINGS

FAST FACT: Calvin Johnson was selected by voters to appear on the cover of EA Sports' *Madden NFL 13* video game.

SUPER STAT

8

RECORD NUMBER OF CONSECUTIVE GAMES IN WHICH JOHNSON HAD 100-PLUS RECEIVING YARDS; TIED BY ADAM THIELEN IN 2018

Who has the record for most receiving yards in one season?

The Detroit Lions entered the 2007 NFL Draft having selected a wide receiver among the top 10 overall picks in three of the previous four drafts. So even though Georgia Tech wideout **CALVIN JOHNSON** was considered one of the top talents coming out of college in 2007, many felt that the Lions might not risk using yet another high draft pick on a receiver. After all, both Charles Rogers (the second overall pick in 2003) and Mike Williams (the 10th overall pick in 2005) turned out to be busts.

The Lions ended up drafting Johnson, and Detroit fans were certainly glad they did. In only his second pro season, he tied for the NFL lead with 12 receiving touchdowns and ranked fifth with 1,331 receiving yards. In 2011, Johnson established himself as the best at his position, leading NFL wideouts with 1,681 yards and 16 touchdowns. He was even better in 2012, leading the league with 122 receptions and setting an NFL single-season record with 1,964 receiving yards, shattering Jerry Rice's previous mark of 1,848.

Along the way, Johnson picked up one of the game's most memorable nicknames. His dominance led to him being called "Megatron." He played three more seasons, topping 1,000 receiving yards each time. However, he retired in 2015. In 2021, he was an easy pick as a new member of the Pro Football Hall of Fame.

DID YOU KNOW?

When Calvin Johnson was a rookie in 2007, his teammate Roy Williams gave him the nickname "Megatron" after seeing the movie *Transformers*. "He catches everything, he's so big, jumps out of this world," Williams said. "He had the visor, and I put it all together, and I'm like, 'He's Megatron.' I said it one day in an interview, and it just stuck."

Who was the first quarterback to rush for 1,000 yards in a season?

Atlanta's **MICHAEL VICK** did something in 2006 that no other quarterback had done before: He rushed for more than 1,000 yards in one season. Playing for the Atlanta Falcons, he gained 1,039 yards on 123 carries. That averages out to 8.45 yards per rush, which is an NFL single-season record, regardless of position. It broke a mark that had been set in 1934 by Chicago Bears running back Beattie Feathers. If you think that is impressive, consider this: As a quarterback, Vick rushed for more career yards than Gale Sayers, who was one of the best running backs ever!

Who is the only player to lead the NFL in rushing for five straight seasons?

Few have ever moved the chains as effectively as **JIM BROWN** did. The star running back spent his entire NFL career with the Cleveland Browns, and his bruising style helped him lead the league in rushing for five straight seasons, starting in 1957. After Jim Taylor of the Green Bay Packers took the title in 1962, Brown led the NFL again for another three straight years. He set a team record for most rushing yards in one season with 1,863 in 1963.

On the NFL's 100th anniversary in 2020, NFL.com ranked Brown as the best running back in NFL history. His career average of 104.3 yards per game is the highest mark of all-time.

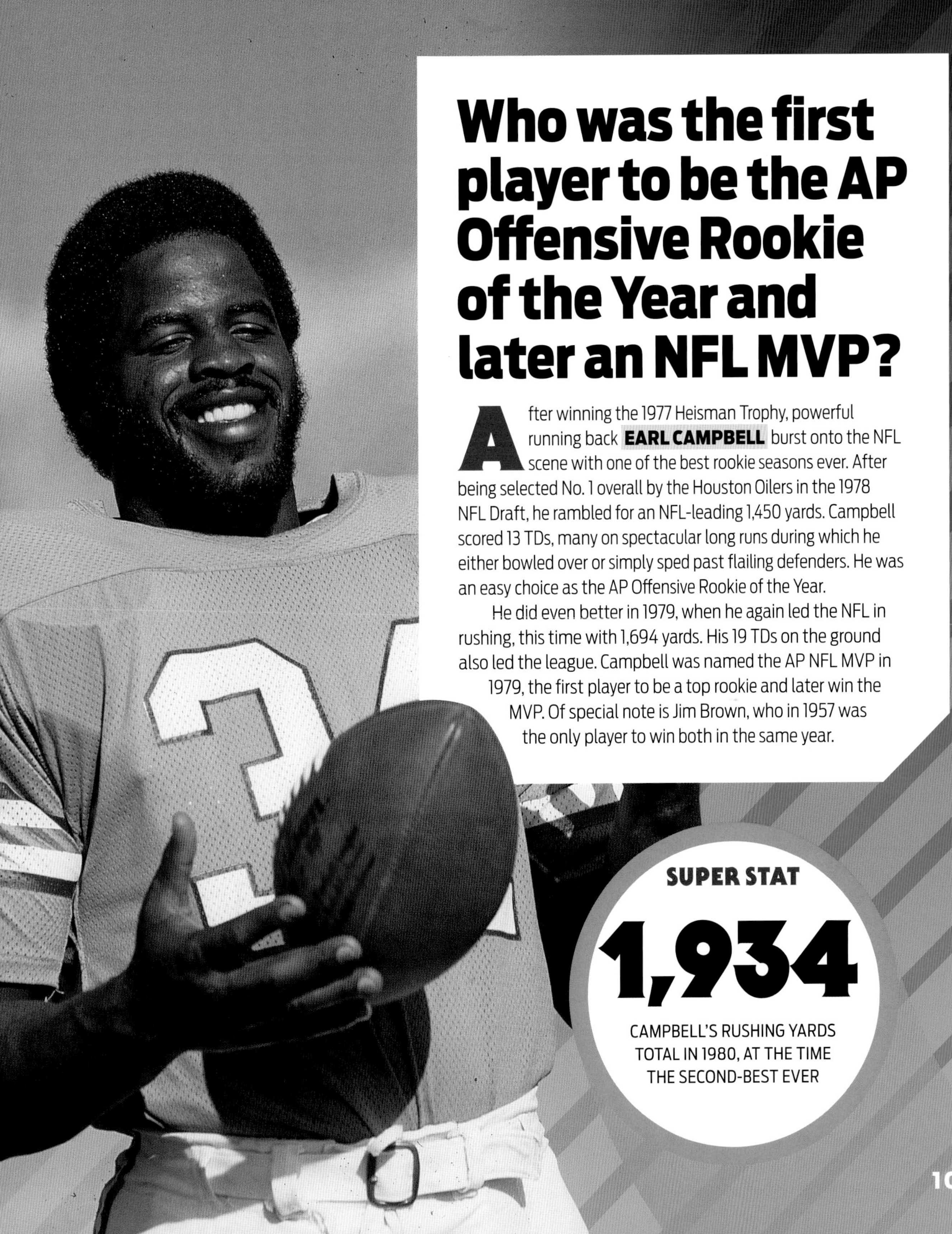

Who was the first player to be the AP Offensive Rookie of the Year and later an NFL MVP?

After winning the 1977 Heisman Trophy, powerful running back **EARL CAMPBELL** burst onto the NFL scene with one of the best rookie seasons ever. After being selected No. 1 overall by the Houston Oilers in the 1978 NFL Draft, he rambled for an NFL-leading 1,450 yards. Campbell scored 13 TDs, many on spectacular long runs during which he either bowled over or simply sped past flailing defenders. He was an easy choice as the AP Offensive Rookie of the Year.

He did even better in 1979, when he again led the NFL in rushing, this time with 1,694 yards. His 19 TDs on the ground also led the league. Campbell was named the AP NFL MVP in 1979, the first player to be a top rookie and later win the MVP. Of special note is Jim Brown, who in 1957 was the only player to win both in the same year.

SUPER STAT

1,934

CAMPBELL'S RUSHING YARDS TOTAL IN 1980, AT THE TIME THE SECOND-BEST EVER

SUPER STAT

2

NUMBER OF TIMES FOSTER LED THE NFL IN TOUCHDOWNS OVER HIS FIRST FOUR SEASONS (2010 AND 2012)

Who holds the record for most rushing yards in one season by an undrafted player?

People doubted Houston Texans running back **ARIAN FOSTER** for a long time. When he said in his seventh grade class that he wanted to grow up to become an NFL player, his teacher suggested that he should come up with a different answer. She thought it wasn't realistic for a kid to expect to become a professional football player.

"I took offense to that, because that's what I wanted to be," Foster said. "I want to inspire any kid out there . . . that if you really focus and you really put everything you have into it, you can do whatever you want to in this world."

Foster gained a reputation for his intense workout regimen and strict diet, and both paid off. Though he was a starter at the University of Tennessee, Foster was not selected in the NFL Draft. He ended up spending most of 2009 on the Texans' practice squad. He exploded onto the scene the following season, leading the NFL with 16 rushing TDs and 1,616 rushing yards, breaking Priest Holmes's single-season record for most rushing yards by an undrafted player. Foster's 1,424 rushing yards in 2014 is the fifth-most of all-time for an undrafted player. After another great season in 2012, injuries slowed his progress. Foster retired during the 2016 season with Miami. He has become an actor, rapper, and podcaster.

FAST FACT: Arian Foster is the only player ever to gain 100 or more rushing yards in each of his first three NFL post-season games.

DID YOU KNOW?

Arian Foster scored three touchdowns and set a single-game team record with 231 rushing yards in the Houston Texans' 34–24 victory over the Indianapolis Colts on September 12, 2010. He became the first player in league history to run for three touchdowns and more than 200 yards on the opening weekend of an NFL season.

Who has the most yards from scrimmage in a season?

In 2009, Tennessee Titans running back **CHRIS JOHNSON** became the sixth player ever to rush for more than 2,000 in a season when he tallied 2,006. He also gained 503 yards on 50 receptions, giving him an NFL single-season record of 2,509 yards from scrimmage.

Johnson was named NFL Offensive Player of the Year for his efforts. With three TD runs of 85 or more yards in 2009 (91, 89, 85), he became the first player ever to register three career touchdown runs of 85 or more yards. No other NFL player had even one run of more than 80 yards in 2009.

SUPER STAT

6

NFL-RECORD NUMBER OF TOUCHDOWNS OF 80 OR MORE YARDS FOR WHICH JOHNSON RAN

SUPER STAT

14

NUMBER OF CONSECUTIVE GAMES IN WHICH SANDERS RAN FOR 100 OR MORE YARDS, AN NFL RECORD HE SET IN 1997

Who is the only player to rush for 1,500 or more yards in four straight NFL seasons?

Few, if any, NFL running backs have been as electrifying over a four-year period as **BARRY SANDERS** was for the Detroit Lions from 1994 to '97. He had consecutive seasons of 1,883, 1,500, 1,553, and 2,053 rushing yards to become the first player in league history with four straight years of at least 1,500 rushing yards.

Sanders is only 5'8", but he made up for his lack of size with impressive leg strength and remarkable quickness. He was so elusive in the open field that defenders who tried to tackle him were often left lunging at air as Sanders raced in a different direction. Sanders was named NFL Offensive Player of the Year in both 1994 and '97.

Who is the running back with the most receiving yards in his NFL career?

The offense that was known as "The Greatest Show on Turf" would never have gotten the big top off the ground without one of the game's most versatile and productive players: **MARSHALL FAULK**. Faulk was traded from the Indianapolis Colts to the St. Louis Rams in 1999. That year, he teamed with quarterback **KURT WARNER**, and receivers Isaac Bruce and Torry Holt, to form one of the most potent offenses the NFL has ever known. The '99 Rams led the league with 526 points, which at the time was the third-highest total in NFL history. The 2000 Rams turned out to be even more explosive, leading the NFL with 540 points in 16 regular-season games.

One of the keys to St. Louis's aerial attack was Faulk's ability to make big plays as a receiver out of the backfield. He caught 80 or more passes for five straight seasons from 1998 to 2002. His 7-yard reception from Rams quarterback Ryan Fitzpatrick in the fourth quarter of a game against the Minnesota Vikings on December 11, 2005 broke the record Larry Centers had set for most career receiving yards by a running back.

Faulk ended his career after the 2005 season with 6,875 receiving yards. The first player in NFL history to gain 2,000 yards from scrimmage in four straight seasons (1998-2001), he retired as the ninth-ranked rusher of all-time with 12,279 yards. In 2011, he was inducted into the Pro Football Hall of Fame.

SUPER STAT

3

NUMBER OF TIMES FAULK WAS NAMED NFL OFFENSIVE PLAYER OF THE YEAR, INCLUDING IN 2000, WHEN HE WAS NAMED NFL MVP

DID YOU KNOW?

FAST FACT: The seven two-point conversions Marshall Faulk made during his career is an NFL record.

Marshall Faulk was held to only 17 rushing yards by the Tennessee Titans in Super Bowl XXXIV, in January 2000. He did catch five passes for 90 yards, and the Rams led by seven points when the Titans got the ball back for one last drive. Tennessee moved the ball to the St. Louis 10-yard line with six seconds remaining. On what would turn out to be the game's final play, quarterback Steve McNair completed a pass to receiver Kevin Dyson, who was tackled one yard short of the goal line by Rams linebacker Mike Jones as time expired. The Rams won the game, 23–16.

Who has the most all-purpose yards in one season?

A "Mr. Everything" for three NFL teams, **DARREN SPROLES** put it all together for an NFL record with the New Orleans Saints. Sproles was always a shifty runner capable of helping his team in a lot of ways. In 2011, he set a new NFL best for most all-purpose yards in one season. All-purpose yards includes those a player gets rushing, receiving, and on kickoff and punt returns. Sproles rushed for a career-best 603 yards in 2011, and he gained 710 receiving yards on passes he caught from quarterback Drew Brees. Sproles finished second among NFL players in kickoff return yards with 1,089, and he gained 294 yards on punt returns for a total of 2,696 all-purpose yards.

Sproles joined the Philadelphia Eagles before the 2014 season and earned the first of three Pro Bowl selections. He retired after the 2019 season.

SUPER STAT

66

SPROLES'S HEIGHT IN INCHES, WHICH MADE THE 5' 6" RUNNING BACK THE SHORTEST PLAYER TO GAIN A YARD IN AN NFL GAME

SUPER STAT

16

GONZALEZ'S TOTAL OF SEASONS WITH AT LEAST 50 RECEPTIONS, MOST BY ANY TIGHT END IN NFL HISTORY

Who has the most career receiving yards for a tight end?

Hall of Famer **TONY GONZALEZ** is not only one of the greatest receiving tight ends in NFL history, his career numbers rank among those of the game's greatest wide receivers. He ended his 17-season career with 15,127 career receiving yards, which is by far the most ever by a tight end. It also ranks sixth among all players on the NFL's all-time list. The next tight end on the list is Jason Witten, whose 13,046 career yards ranks 20th on that same list.

Gonzalez played basketball in college at the University of California, and he often used the skills he developed on the hardwood to get an edge in the end zone. He would use his size and strength to box out defensive backs, shielding them off with his body as if getting in position for a rebound. Other times, he outleaped defenders to snatch the ball at its highest point. Those skills helped Gonzalez become one of only 10 players in NFL history to catch more than 100 career touchdown passes.

Who holds the mark for longest kick return?

On the first play of a 2013 game between the Minnesota Vikings and the Green Bay Packers, **CORDARRELLE PATTERSON** of the Vikings broke the record for the longest kick return in NFL history with a 109-yard return for a touchdown. The run tied the record for the longest play, set in 2007 by Antonio Cromartie on a missed field goal. Jacksonville's Jamal Agnew matched both players with a field-goal miss return in a 2021 game.

FAST FACT: Andrew Luck's seven game-winning drives in the fourth quarter or overtime in 2012 were the most ever by a rookie quarterback.

Who has the record for most passing yards by a rookie?

When **ANDREW LUCK** was selected by the Indianapolis Colts with the first pick of the 2012 NFL Draft, he immediately had big shoes to fill. Peyton Manning had been the team's top overall pick in the 1998 draft, and was a star for many years. But Manning left the Colts and signed with the Denver Broncos a month prior to the 2012 draft.

Luck rewarded the Colts' confidence in him by leading them to an 11–5 record. He gave fans in Indianapolis an early Christmas gift by securing a 20–13 victory over the Kansas City Chiefs on December 23. The win clinched a spot in the playoffs with one game left in the season for a team that had gone 2–14 the previous year. In the game's second quarter, Luck broke Cam Newton's rookie record of 4,051 passing yards. Luck ended the season with 4,374 yards.

Who has rushed for the most yards in one quarter?

Running back **JAMAAL CHARLES** rushed for more yards in the third quarter of a game against the New Orleans Saints on September 23, 2012, than some good running backs rush for in two games! His 162 yards in that quarter included a 91-yard touchdown that cut the Saints' lead to 24–13, and it sparked the Chiefs' impressive comeback. Kansas City would outscore New Orleans 11–0 in the fourth quarter and go on to win, 27–24, on a field goal in overtime.

The win over the Saints was one of the few highlights for the Chiefs in 2012. Kansas City tied the Jacksonville Jaguars for the worst record in the NFL at 2–14. Charles was the team's bright spot. He became the third Chiefs player to rush for more than 1,500 yards in one season. He also finished 2012 as the NFL's all-time leader for highest career rushing average by a running back with at least 750 attempts: His 4,536 yards on 784 carries equalled a then NFL-best 5.8 yards per carry. Even after he retired in 2018, Charles's final number of 5.4 yards per carry was fifth-most all-time.

SUPER STAT

80

IN 2012, CHARLES JOINED BARRY SANDERS AND CHRIS JOHNSON AS THE ONLY PLAYERS WITH THREE 80-PLUS YARD RUNS IN A YEAR

SUPER STAT

444

KAEPERNICK'S NUMBER OF COMBINED YARDS IN HIS RECORD-SETTING PERFORMANCE AGAINST THE PACKERS

Who has the most rushing yards by a quarterback in one game?

Many people questioned San Francisco 49ers head coach Jim Harbaugh's decision to replace starting quarterback Alex Smith with backup **COLIN KAEPERNICK** in the middle of the 2012 regular season. After all, Smith had led the 49ers to the NFC Championship Game after the 2011 season.

The gamble paid off. In the first post-season start of his career, Kaepernick led the 49ers to a 45–31 win over the Green Bay Packers. His 181 rushing yards in that game set an NFL record for quarterbacks, in the regular season or playoffs. It topped the previous mark of 173 yards set by Michael Vick on December 1, 2002.

FAST FACT: As part of his post-career activism about equality, Kaepernick became a children's book author!

DID YOU KNOW?

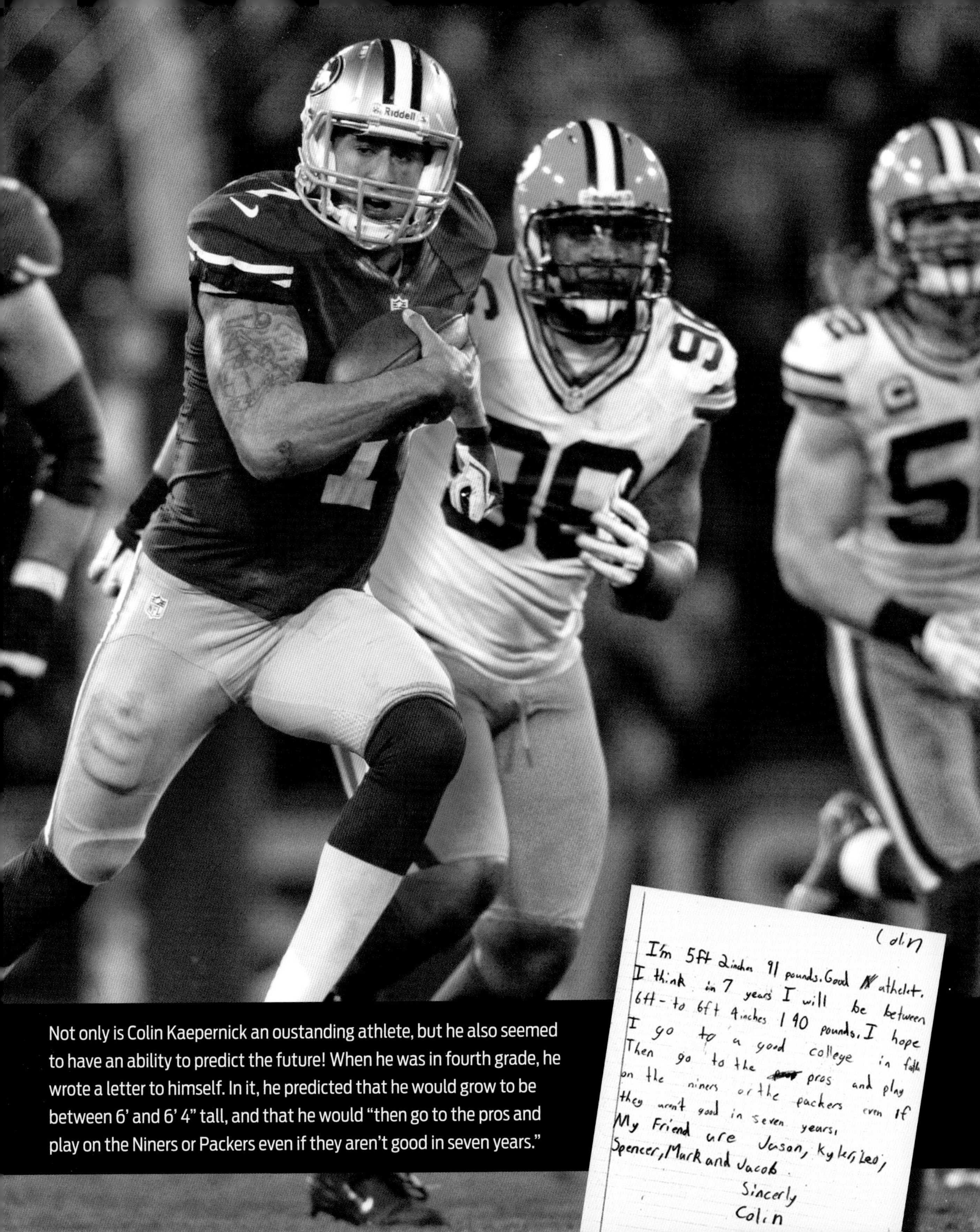

Not only is Colin Kaepernick an oustanding athlete, but he also seemed to have an ability to predict the future! When he was in fourth grade, he wrote a letter to himself. In it, he predicted that he would grow to be between 6' and 6' 4" tall, and that he would "then go to the pros and play on the Niners or Packers even if they aren't good in seven years."

SUPER STAT

5

NUMBER OF NFL MOST VALUABLE PLAYER AWARDS MANNING WON IN HIS CAREER, THE MOST IN NFL HISTORY

Who has the record for most seasons with 4,000 or more passing yards?

When **PEYTON MANNING** missed the 2011 season after undergoing four neck surgeries, many questioned whether he would ever be as great as he had been for the Indianapolis Colts, for whom he had 11 seasons with 4,000-plus passing yards (and, of course, a Super Bowl win). The Denver Broncos had no such doubts, signing Manning to a five-year contract once the Colts released him after the 2011 season. He went on to do everything he could to prove that he was as dominant as ever—and cement his place as one of the greatest players of all-time.

With Denver, Manning had three more 4,000-yard seasons to set the NFL record of 14. One of those was good for another record: the single-season passing yards mark of 5,477 yards. He still held both marks when he was inducted into the Pro Football Hall of Fame in 2021.

Who has the most interceptions in a single season?

There have been a lot of great defensive backs in the NFL in the past 70 years since **DICK "NIGHT TRAIN" LANE** made his incredible NFL debut. NFL teams now play more games and throw many times more passes than in those days, while players are faster, stronger, and have better ways to train and learn. Even so, in all those seasons and with all those footballs flying around, no one has topped the still-standing NFL record of 14 interceptions in one season that Night Train set in 1952. Incredibly, it was his rookie season, too. And he set the mark in what was then only a 12-game season! Lane's path to the Pro Football Hall of Fame, to which he was elected in 1974, was unusual. He had been in the Army and played only junior college football before asking for a tryout with the Rams. Impressed by his athletic skills, the team turned him from a receiver to a defensive back. Lane then lit up the league to start his amazing career.

SUPER STAT

68

LANE'S CAREER TOTAL OF INTERCEPTIONS, STILL GOOD FOR FOURTH ALL-TIME

Who led the NFL in rushing yards in 2021?

When the 2021 NFL season began, fantasy football fans knew that **JONATHAN TAYLOR** was the Colts' starting running back and might be worth a mid-round pick. When the season was over, they were sorry they had waited! As a rookie in 2020, he had had a solid season, scoring 11 TDs and rushing for 1,169 yards. And in the 2021 season's first eight games, it looked like more of the same—solid but not spectacular. In Week 9, however, in Indy's 45–30 win over the Jets, Taylor burst for 172 rushing yards, a season high until two weeks later when he ran for 185 yards and four touchdowns as the Colts shocked the Buffalo Bills 41–15. In the second half of the season, Taylor had 100-yard totals in seven of nine games and scored in all but two games. He wound up leading the NFL with 1,811 rushing yards and 18 rushing TDs. He'll be higher ranked in fantasy in 2022!

SUPER STAT

2,171

TAYLOR'S NFL-LEADING YARDS FROM SCRIMMAGE TOTAL, WITH 360 RECEIVING YARDS TO GO WITH HIS 1,811 RUSHING YARDS

FAST FACT: Roger Craig's 92 receptions in 1985 led all NFL players. He remains the last running back ever to lead the NFL in receptions for a single season.

Who was first to reach 1,000 rushing and 1,000 receiving yards in one NFL season?

San Francisco 49ers coach Bill Walsh was very wise when he said in 1983 that "**ROGER CRAIG** is going to become a great football player very soon." At the time, Craig was in his first training camp with the team after being a second-round pick in the NFL Draft. In 1984, Craig led the 49ers with 71 receptions even though he was a running back. He ended the season by becoming the first player ever to score three touchdowns in a Super Bowl, which he did during the 49ers' 38–16 win over the Miami Dolphins. The following year, Craig became the first player ever to reach 1,000 rushing yards and 1,000 receiving yards in the same NFL season. Coach Walsh sure called that one!

Who has the Packers' record for most career passing yards?

When he retired in 2010, the great **BRETT FAVRE** held most of the NFL's important career passing records. He was tops in passing yards and touchdown passes. Those records have since fallen, but Favre still holds a couple of key marks. He set an NFL record by starting 297 straight regular-season games between September 1992 and December 2010. That's one record that figures to stand for a while. One of his marks that might fall is the Packers' career passing yards total, with 61,655. Favre's replacement in Green Bay, Aaron Rodgers, is closing in at 55,360, but Favre is still on top.

SUPER STAT

4,544

JOSH ALLEN'S PASSING YARDS TOTAL FOR 2020, SETTING A NEW BUFFALO BILLS' SINGLE-SEASON RECORD

FAST FACT: A fun bit of trivia: What NFL QB was sacked in 2021 by a player with the same name as him? Buffalo QB Josh Allen was taken down by Jacksonville Jaguars LB Josh Allen!

Who is the only player in NFL history with 4,000 passing yards, 30 TD passes, and 8 TD runs in one season?

When **JOSH ALLEN** joined the Buffalo Bills in 2018, he was seen as a strong-armed passer from the University of Wyoming. For a BIlls team that had been struggling for years, could he be a game-changer? His rookie season showed signs of promise, but also revealed his all-around skills. He threw only 10 TD passes, but he ran for eight scores. His talents just kept getting better. He had nine rushing TDs in 2019, while doubling his TD passes. It was in 2020 that he really emerged as one of the NFL's best players. With 4,544 passing yards, 37 touchdown passes, and eight TD runs, he became the first player ever with the stat line of this question. More importantly for Bills fans, Allen has turned out to be the leader the team needed. Starting in 2019, they reached the playoffs three straight seasons, the first time the team had done that since 1993. Allen hopes to add a Super Bowl championship to his growing list of accomplishments.

DID YOU KNOW

Bills fans will never forget the epic 2022 AFC Divisional Playoff. It was one of the instant classic games in NFL history—but it was one the Bills ultimately lost. After Kansas City went ahead with a minute left, Allen led a drive to a go-ahead score with 13 seconds left. Somehow, the Chiefs tied the score in that time and went on to win in an overtime period in which Allen and the Bills didn't even touch the ball. Allen did set a record that he would certainly swap for a victory—the first player in NFL history with back-to-back playoff games with four TD passes and no interceptions.

PLAYER INDEX

BIG
BOOK OF
WHO
FOOTBALL

PHOTO CREDITS

Cover: Illustration by Artistic Image / AA Reps Inc.
Front Cover: David E. Klutho for Sports Illustrated (Patrick Mahomes); John Iacono for Sports Illustrated (Emmitt Smith); Erick W. Rasco for Sports Illustrated (Tom Brady)
Back Cover: Al Tielemans for Sports Illustrated (Aaron Rodgers); Simon Bruty for Sports Illustrated (Derrick Henry); Erick W. Rasco for Sports Illustrated (Justin Herbert); Andy Hayt for Sports Illustrated (Joe Montana)
Page 3: David E. Klutho for Sports Illustrated (Patrick Mahomes, Christian McCaffrey); Bill Frakes for Sports Illustrated (Ray Lewis); Scott W. Grau/ Icon Sportswire via AP Photo (Justin Tucker); Al Tielemans for Sports Illustrated (Chris Johnson)
Pages 4-5: Bill Frakes for Sports Illustrated (Russell Wilson); Damian Strohmeyer for Sports Illustrated (Eli Manning); David E. Klutho for Sports Illustrated (Patrick Mahomes); Andy Hayt for Sports Illustrated (Joe Montana)
Pages 6-7: David E. Klutho for Sports Illustrated
Pages 8-9: Neil Leifer for Sports Illustrated (Bart Starr); Damian Strohmeyer for Sports Illustrated (Eli Manning); Al Tielemans for Sports Illustrated (Aaron Rodgers)
Pages 10-11: Hy Peskin for Sports Illustrated
Pages 12-13: Andy Hayt for Sports Illustrated (Joe Montana); Neil Leifer for Sports Illustrated (Terry Bradshaw)
Pages 14-15: David E. Klutho for Sports Illustrated
Pages 16-17: Andy Hayt for Sports Illustrated (Phil Simms); John Iacono for Sports Illustrated (Emmitt Smith, Terrell Davis)
Pages 18-19: John W. McDonough for Sports Illustrated
Pages 20-21: Simon Bruty for Sports Illustrated (Michael Vick, Tom Brady); John Iacono for Sports Illustrated (Desmond Howard)
Pages 22-23: Al Tielemans for Sports Illustrated
Pages 24-25: John Iacono for Sports Illustrated (Steve Young); Bill Frakes for Sports Illustrated (Adam Vinatieri); John Biever for Sports Illustrated (James Harrison)
Pages 26-27: Simon Bruty for Sports Illustrated
Pages 28-29: Neil Leifer for Sports Illustrated (Joe Namath); Bill Frakes for Sports Illustrated (Russell Wilson)
Pages 30-31: Simon Bruty for Sports Illustrated (Derrick Henry); David E. Klutho for Sports Illustrated (Joe Burrow); Al Tielemans for Sports Illustrated (Deion Sanders); Bill Frakes for Sports Illustrated (Ray Lewis)
Pages 32-33: Simon Bruty for Sports Illustrated
Pages 34-35: John Iacono for Sports Illustrated (Jim McMahon); AP Photo (Norman "Boomer" Esiason); Damian Strohmeyer for Sports Illustrated (Jerome Bettis)
Pages 36-37: David E. Klutho for Sports Illustrated
Pages 38-39: Heinz Kluetmeier for Sports Illustrated (Walter Payton); Andy Hayt for Sports Illustrated (Cris Collinsworth)
Pages 40-41: Al Tielemans for Sports Illustrated
Pages 42-43: Fred Vuich for Sports Illustrated (Cleveland Browns); Jeff Haynes for Sports Illustrated (Green Bay Packers)
Pages 44-45: Andy Hayt for Sports Illustrated (Brian Bosworth); John Iacono for Sports Illustrated (Ickey Woods)
Pages 46-47: Bill Frakes for Sports Illustrated
Pages 48-49: Damian Strohmeyer for Sports Illustrated (Chad Johnson); Simon Bruty for Sports Illustrated (Tyrann Mathieu)
Pages 50-51: Andy Hayt for Sports Illustrated (Bo Jackson); Heinz Kluetmeier for Sports Illustrated (William Perry)
Pages 52-53: John W. McDonough for Sports Illustrated
Pages 54-55: John W. McDonough for Sports Illustrated (Larry Fitzgerald, George Kittle); Four Seams Images via AP Images (Bruce Smith); Simon Bruty for Sports Illustrated (Mike Evans)
Pages 56-57: David E. Klutho for Sports Illustrated
Pages 58-59: Damian Strohmeyer for Sports Illustrated (Devin Hester); Erick W. Rasco for Sports Illustrated (Kyler Murray); John W. McDonough for Sports Illustrated (Larry Fitzgerald)
Pages 60-61: Erick W. Rasco for Sports Illustrated
Pages 62-63: John Biever for Sports Illustrated (Charles Woodson); Erick W. Rasco for Sports Illustrated (Justin Herbert)
Pages 64-65: John Iacono for Sports Illustrated
Pages 66-67: Greg Nelson for Sports Illustrated (Michael Thomas); Simon Bruty for Sports Illustrated (Lamar Jackson)
Pages 68-69: Heinz Kluetmeier for Sports Illustrated (Willie McGinest); Four Seams Images via AP Images (Bruce Smith); John W. McDonough for Sports Illustrated (George Kittle)
Pages 70-71: Simon Bruty for Sports Illustrated
Pages 72-73: Rob Tringali for Sports Illustrated (Zach Ertz); Al Tielemans for Sports Illustrated (Brandon Marshall)
Pages 74-75: Robert Beck for Sports Illustrated (Muhsin Muhammad); Simon Bruty for Sports Illustrated (Charles Tillman); Neil Leifer for Sports Illustrated (Lawrence Taylor)
Pages 76-77: Andy Hayt for Sports Illustrated
Pages 78-79: Heinz Kluetmeier for Sports Illustrated (Jerry Rice); Al Tielemans for Sports Illustrated (Tim Tebow); Scott W. Grau/Icon Sportswire via AP Images (Justin Tucker); AP Photo/Evan Pinkus (Victor Cruz)
Pages 80-81: Al Tielemans for Sports Illustrated
Pages 82-83: Heinz Kluetmeier for Sports Illustrated (Doug Williams); Al Tielemans for Sports Illustrated (Jacoby Jones); AP Photo/Paul Abell (Doug Martin)
Pages 84-85: Neil Leifer for Sports Illustrated (Gale Sayers); Al Tielemans for Sports Illustrated (Rob Gronkowski)
Pages 86-87: Bill Frakes for Sports Illustrated
Pages 88-89: AP Photo/Al Messerschmidt (George Blanda); Andy Hayt for Sports Illustrated (Rod Woodson)
Pages 90-91: AP Photo/David J. Phillip
Pages 92-93: Al Tielemans for Sports Illustrated (Tim Tebow); Scott W. Grau/Icon Sportswire via AP Images (Justin Tucker)
Pages 94-95: Heinz Kluetmeier for Sports Illustrated
Pages 96-97: John W. McDonough for Sports Illustrated (LaDainian Tomlinson); AP Photo/Evan Pinkus (Victor Cruz)
Pages 98-99: Bob Rosato for Sports Illustrated (Randy Moss); Simon Bruty for Sports Illustrated (Ben Roethlisberger); Al Tielemans via AP (Jake Elliott)
Pages 100-101: Simon Bruty for Sports Illustrated
Pages 102-103: Bob Rosato for Sports Illustrated (Brett Favre); John W. McDonough for Sports Illustrated (Calvin Johnson); Erick W. Rasco for Sports Illustrated (Josh Allen); Al Tielemans for Sports Illustrated (Chris Johnson)
Pages 104-105: John W. McDonough for Sports Illustrated
Pages 106-107: Heinz Kluetmeier for Sports Illustrated (Earl Campbell); Neil Leifer for Sports Illustrated (Jim Brown)
Pages 108-109: Damian Strohmeyer for Sports Illustrated
Pages 110-111: Al Tielemans for Sports Illustrated (Chris Johnson); John Iacono for Sports Illustrated (Barry Sanders)
Pages 112-113: John W. McDonough for Sports Illustrated
Pages 114-115: Bill Frakes for Sports Illustrated (Darren Sproles); Al Tielemans for Sports Illustrated (Tony Gonzalez)
Pages 116-117: AP Photo/Kiichiro Sato (Cordarrelle Patterson); David E. Klutho for Sports Illustrated (Andrew Luck); AP Photo/Gerald Herbert (Jamaal Charles)
Pages 118-119: John W. McDonough for Sports Illustrated
Pages 120-121: David E. Klutho for Sports Illustrated (Peyton Manning); AP Photo/Harold P. Matosian (Dick Lane)
Pages 122-123: Icon Sportswire via AP Images (Jonathan Taylor); Andy Hayt for Sports Illustrated (Roger Craig); Bob Rosato for Sports Illustrated (Brett Favre)
Pages 124-125: Erick W. Rasco for Sports Illustrated